QHHT AND BQH PRACTITIONERS

EXPLORE the SHIFT to NEW EARTH

Merging from 3D Carbon to
5D Crystalline bodies

Conversations with Heaven on Earth - YouTube
I'm that Girl - YouTube

the SHIFT to NEW EARTH

the SHIFT to NEW EARTH

The butterfly does not mourn its caterpillar phase.

the SHIFT to NEW EARTH

This book has been edited by many incredible humans who are of service FOR YOU.

They have worked hard to edit the verbal messages from sessions into a smooth and easy to read format.

You are welcome to listen to the original sessions for the ones which are public to hear.

As we have been guided to remind you – reading this information – you will be able to absorb the content easily.

To honor all who worked on this book freely for you, it would be most respectful and appreciated if <u>you can apply the information into your daily life, which would empower you in the most profound of ways</u>.

As each person was guided to edit the sessions, their format felt appropriate for them. Accepting others' approaches is part of our inner work to accept and respect all. Do not get distracted by the details ~ focus on the concepts given.

You are very much loved and have been guided to this information at a very important time for humanity, this planet and for your soul experience here on Earth ~ in honor of Mastering Human.

Please write the page numbers for the chapters when you finish reading in the Table of Contents

the SHIFT to NEW EARTH

Table of Contents

Introduction ....
Dolores's Message to Practitioners ....
Session 1 ....
Session 2 ....
Session 3 ....
Session 4 ....
Session 5 ....
Session 6 ....
Session 7 ....
Session 8 ....
Session 9 ....
Session 10 ....
Summary Session ....
Farewell note ....
Important Reminder for All ....
Reminders for Clients Seeking Practitioners ......
What to Look for in a Practitioner ....

Introduction

This book contains a recent series of quantum sessions asking the same questions with 10 people, mostly QHHT and BQH practitioners, located around the world[1]. You can read their higher version of self being channeled through their 3D bodies, answering questions that their conscious mind did not know was going to be asked from them. Each client was asked similar questions, as this is a series about exploring the shift of the carbon-based bodies into the crystalline-based bodies. As we explore this, we learn what New Earth and being in 5D actually means from higher dimensional beings.

Each session starts off exploring how the body of the client is doing. This is a great insight into what is truly going on for the person and a direct reflection of any of their underlying inner work. This is important not only for the client to know, but also for the reader to gain a sense of how the person is living their life.

The questions are not only a very important part of this technique, but also to know if the client has major inner work they need to address. Any remaining inner work seems to stop the Subconscious (main guide, or over soul) from wanting to explore these questions, as the client needs to focus on their inner work to be ready for

---

[1] While they knew these sessions could be used publicly, they all remain anonymous for the purpose of this book.

this level of information. The Subconscious knows what the clients are ready to know and if they are able to handle this information.

The clients were invited to be a part of this series, and they do not know each other privately. While most are practitioners for BQH and/or QHHT, they are also mostly First and Second Wave Volunteers.

This is a profound recent series for those people seeking this advanced information. The series was released publicly, all at once, and even the clients got to hear the other sessions at the same time as everyone else was able to. All sessions were done within six days of starting the project. While we hear from people using their human mindsets talking about the shift to 5D being here on this planet— we do not actually hear that in either QHHT or BQH sessions. We invite all practitioners to ask the same questions when they have their next session as a client themself. For anyone who has a collective that cannot shift to the 5th Dimension, this might be a good concept to explore and ask why. Not all collectives can shift into the 5th Dimension at this point, such as the Reptilian starseeds, as each collective wants to evolve together. Not all can evolve at the same rate. For the souls who have Earth as their home planet, this shift is an important part of their soul's journey. All volunteers who are here to support beings here on Earth need to do this without judgment, with maturity and love for all.

It is important to know what you are asking, as labels and names of things can trip us up. Asking if we are shifting with Gaia is not the same as asking if we are shifting with this physical Earth. The Planet is not Gaia, and Gaia is not the Planet. Just like how you are not your body, it is a vehicle for your soul. It is the same for our beloved Gaia and her body incarnated as Earth. Souls have life contracts and live forever, whereas all physical bodies, the vehicles for the souls, have a beginning and an end stage of their journey.

Dolores's Message to Practitioners

Marvelous, thank you, thank you, thank you so much for being able to orchestrate this book from that little experiment. For the series to be conducted in such a way, it was clever. To be able to do a blind study, a blind series for people who you knew were going to be able to do the best they could to push away their human consciousness, their human egos, to be able to channel advanced beings. I was there the entire time assisting with this because I thought, "how extraordinary and remarkable to be able to have this undeniable experience with the New Earth information coming from 10 different vehicles[2], marvelous."

While I didn't do any series like this myself— because I just did not even consider or think that this could be something that would need to be showcased in my books. What I did place into my books was accounts that I had faith and trust in and was of interest to report. The information was validated through others and was correct information for the time we were working in then. I knew the difference between the conscious mind of my clients and that of advanced knowledge from the

---

[2] Souls have free will to come into these sessions if they choose. No one can own or control a soul, and they can speak for themselves. However, we know some people try to block advanced beings' information from being shared publicly. Question everything and explore this in your own Quantum sessions. QHHT interns give 25 free sessions as part of their training.

subconscious, because THEY gave me the answers I was seeking. It always made sense when I asked the right questions and could wrap my human mind around the concepts and information. Of course, some information I did not know how to process and was guided into other areas which THEY wanted me to understand and focus on more. THEY kept me busy, which I loved, and there was always more to explore. If I did get too distracted in one concept, THEY always had a way of redirecting me into the direction which needed to be collected to then share in my books and public talks.

Upon reflection, while there was consistent information, I did not make such a big deal about the fact that I was asking the same questions and getting the same answers consistently in my books. I certainly did not make an entire book highlighting that point, as I felt explaining my process should have been enough for people to understand how this information was collected. There was a point I reached where having to prove this work and information to others felt like a distraction in itself. People were either going to believe it or not. I left that up to them, as I was overall more interested in collecting and reporting the information than how other people were coping to believe this information or not.

As you know, the subjects would translate the information not only in their own language, but also in their own dialogue, their own descriptions, and their own interpretation of the messages. For example, I am now showing her a glass of dark brown liquid, sparkly fluid, and I am saying to the vehicle, "What is this drink?" and the vehicle is saying, "I hope it's my favorite— Pepsi Max Vanilla— Pepsi Max is sugar-free, that's quite delicious, and I quite appreciate that on occasions," and I am saying to her, "It is my favorite drink, and this is not the same, but this is your interpretation and perspective from translating and explaining the message." This is how channeling should be understood and why it is always important to have follow-up questions to make sure the messages are being understood through the vehicle/clients/subjects. Therefore, I have just shown the reader this concept through representing how the vehicle can assume information. She has been shown merely a glass of sparkly, fizzy, dark, brown, drink that is the undeniable, recognizable form of Cola drink. However, is it Pepsi? Is it Coca-Cola? And what flavor is it? And Dolores is saying, "You've got much more variety than I had". She is saying this is a classic example of how one vehicle could assume what that fluid was representing. I could tell her now that this fluid is not representing a true hydration or nourishment of the body, and that water is going to be more uplifting to her than any caffeinated, carbonated, and sugary drink. The vehicle was again saying, "Well, it is sugar-free, does that count for anything?" and Dolores replied "not in my books", so there is that.

This is just a conversation between two dear soul friends who are acknowledging each other's energy fields, and it is quite blissful[3]. In fact, it is making the vehicle cry, and Dolores's soul energy knows this frequency is so familiar that this can cause emotions for the channeler. As they are such dear soul family, dear soul friends, and the frequency energy is so familiar with each other, the energy signature frequency of Dolores knows to keep a distance while being channeled, to be here but not to present herself fully energetically, because it will break down the vehicle completely, emotionally[4]. Dolores was just testing that because the vehicle says, "No, that's fine. I'm brave, I don't do that. I don't cry. I haven't cried over you for ages." And so, the signature frequency energy of Dolores just showed the vehicle once again that she was absolutely right, absolutely right, always absolutely right[5].

The vehicle is appreciative of the comfort of this soul frequency energy because it is very familiar and reassuring. But also, the vehicle is saying, "Well, why did you do that? Now I've got to focus on channeling and the emotions are bringing my consciousness too close." This is why Dolores is now saying, "Well, yes, I wanted to

---

[3] Around this point in the channeling, the Arcturian, which is the vehicle's subconscious, came into the conversation.
[4] Dolores moved her energy field closer to the vehicle, which had an instant emotional outburst reaction. As the vehicle was doubting she would be affected by the energy, she was wrong. Dolores was very much right.
[5] Many tears of love and gratitude were released. For people who know the vehicle, this session was 'snot bubble city'!

prove to you that if I am too close it does have that reaction. The body does have that reaction and it is fine, but I wanted to reassure the vehicle that all is well."

I want people to know that this is my work. I am still trying to impress upon others to grow with this, but this book is not just my work, this is our work, this is all of humanity's work, and it always was meant to be. I understand the passion and dedication that the soul within the vehicle has towards me because of our other connections. This has given great honor and drive to honor myself in that lifetime as being Dolores, with pure integrity, but the vehicle has not realized her own positioning in this work, in this teamwork. We're all here, we're all here. She is included in helping humanity. It is like she hasn't truly recognized her role in this as well. She is looking up towards me and my feat. While I did the best I could, there was no one else who was supposed to be me. She is perfectly being herself, and that is marvelous, and that is so necessary. She is incorruptible, and she does not succumb to peer pressure, where I have seen many other practitioners who have succumbed to peer pressure. Because they are not using this work to their full advantage in terms of asking the right questions and can only assume certain things because of other controlling factors, such as influences and practitioners.

When you understand that all the collectives here, all the species, all the other beings, where you originated from, where you are of service to still, are all watching this

Earth show. When you have paused your life from other planets to come here to be of service, to volunteer, to have these brief moments in time, a dream within a dream of lives here on Earth. Many of you are going back to those lifetimes— to continue on with living those that you did live before you came to volunteer to be here for Earth, to be here for Gaia and humanity— after your own shift.

For all of those different aspects, from different planets and those different lives, you could even say spaceships that you were all participating in working amongst, within and beyond, you are all getting your own unique collective accountability of lessons and experiences and your interpretation of what could be in that glass which could be Coca-Cola. It depends on your collective. It really doesn't matter at all— it is the same, but when you are looking at the Earth experience and what happened here on Earth, each collective is going to have its own recollection records. While it's all the same, the glass is the same in terms of Earth always being the same. Different collectives will have different flavors they would like for their vehicles to experience and have assumptions of what is in the glass. It becomes very convoluted quickly when you're realizing that many collectives are having simultaneous experiences of what you perceive in your time, but yet quite different. While there isn't really that much difference between Coca-Cola and Pepsi in terms of flavor or taste or price, there is a subtle difference[6]. When you're exploring the

the SHIFT to NEW EARTH

differences between the different collectives with their experiences here on Earth, it is perfect for each different variant and experience. While it's subtly different between each collective and is significant for their lessons and growth and journey on Earth moving forward, when you all shift, regardless of whether you're going to the New Earth or you're going back to home planets; eventually you will all still share the story and lessons of Earth. This is one story that needs to be honored and shared universally because this never should happen again. What has been allowed upon Earth must never truly be allowed to get to this extent ever again. The lessons must be learned here, and there is therefore no need for it to get out of hand. When you understand the councils, and when you understand what you would call federations, galactic groups and collectives, and there's many committee meetings overseeing the Earth experience, it is like you're at summer camp here on Earth. It's like we are the camp leaders and we're discussing and planning to give you the best opportunities for all the experiences needed to match your life contracts and purpose for being here now— while you're living out your days here. We're trying to plan your days to make sure that you have the best fun, the best opportunities. What we know as your camp leaders is that you're scared to ride the river rapids and you're scared to do the abseiling[7]. You're scared to

---

[6] It is all perspectives, but the difference between orange juice and cola for example is not a subtle difference.

[7] Abseiling is also known as rappelling, or the controlled descent of

do a whole lot of stuff that you've promised that you would come and have the adventure of on Earth. And we as your guides are pushing you daily to face your fears and be adventurous while you're here on Earth. And when you have accumulated so many Earth experiences, you're wrapping and packing up to leave this summer holiday, these lessons, this school of experiences here on Earth. For those who had never been to camp before, which is what you could call a 3D planet, this is a special camp because this is a very challenging one— advanced. It is not a small summer's game. This is an extreme sport where you can say emotionally what you're enduring and exploring here on Earth in its totality; it is very, very advanced, a very challenging game, but it's one you are still playing out. You must be able to understand why you're feeling so stressed, so intensified and so driven to find the truth— to understand, and to know thyself, and to know your soul mission and purpose here on Earth. This is why I want you all to be able to know the tool kits of what you've got, being practitioners and even as clients. You must think cleverly about the questions you're asking and want the practitioner to ask yourselves. Because if you keep it small and ask about smaller things, you may miss the point entirely. You must do enough of your inner work to be ready for the big information. **Most of the volunteers are born into that privilege of just getting the information, regardless of whether they are ready or not.** There is a game called

---

a rock face.

Hide and Seek, and we see some of you are hiding from your inner work, and we're seeking you out, and we're pushing you, and we say this with love because you've forgotten what you promised humanity to be able to do for itself, as you are here as advanced souls. But even advanced souls were not truly prepared for the density of Earth because this game is quite the challenging one. And while I could use human names and labels to describe and define the true game you're within, there is no point dwelling on that.

We can tell that you're all coming together as a team, and it is marvelous. Therefore, seek out important questions. Never just think about how to support your client—consider and think about their family, think about their friends, and their communities, and their locations. While you're trying to help them see and identify what's triggering them this lifetime. You are, as a practitioner, able to find the root issues for all, and so you can call in many Subconsciouses to work through your vehicles. This is marvelous to be able to use your client as a surrogate for all of their friends and family with reason, however, don't overwhelm the vehicle. Don't try to do all of your exploration with your vehicles, with your clients, in one session.

I want to also remind yourselves why you were prompted to do this work and to support humanity. It truly wasn't really about money. It was about helping humanity, and helping humanity shouldn't come at a cost when they are struggling with their finances. Please, please, please, open your hearts to hearing what they have to say and support them. There is nothing more upsetting for us to see— than you dismissing helping humanity because they can't afford it. That is not how you are here to be of service. For those of you who are finding and questioning and wondering why their businesses are not thriving— it's because you've got the wrong priorities. Go back and honor all who find you, without judgment of if they can pay you. Be open to hearing them, and support their healing through them experiencing channeling themselves and learning from their own guides. You have the tools and the keys to be able to do this for them. Trust that when you are of service, you are abundantly rewarded. Don't assume because your clients cannot financially afford sessions, they should not have one with you. You will miss out on much growth yourself with that approach. You still need to support all with sessions or guide them to interns who still honor the service of supporting people in need. You can assume that we will be able to support you in other ways and other means when you do support others who need your help. When you are following your life purpose, you will always be supported in all the things you need, not all the things you want. There is a difference. In your own sessions as a client, ask your own Subconscious if this is even your life purpose doing this work. That would be a great starting point before doing any course.

This is important for you to not be focused on money because money has a different density, and it is not truly uplifting. You should know that knowledge itself is priceless, and these sessions for the practitioners and clients are treasures of extreme wealth in terms of spiritual value. As soon as you start worrying about the lack of anything, including money, your energy falls into density as a low level fear. Fear takes your energy frequency and drops it into a very low vibration. This is not you being of service to humanity at all. Regardless of what you're doing, worrying about anything is not high frequency. You all must focus on how to achieve high frequency, and if you are a practitioner who hasn't done a regular or recent session as a client, this is important for you to maintain your own balance and find what your Subconscious has to say for you. Because sometimes your clients are channeling your own Subconscious telling you what you should be applying— but you are dismissing it because you're thinking it's just for your client. All information from collectives can be applied in honor and respect for them, not just for your clients. So take notice of what you're hearing— there is significance and purpose for all.

It is important to be able to maintain oneself's own inner work, and when you have heard session information, potentially a year ago, and you are applying and assuming that this is current information; I would like to remind you that this is a time of significant events and stages for humanity, and I would encourage all practitioners to find other practitioners to work with. This is supposed to be teamwork. This was never supposed to be an independent competition of practitioners. This was supposed to be friends supporting friends. This was supposed to be a Quantum family, and the more you could support and share with each other— the more this could grow the work profoundly and empower practitioners and all of humanity.

You are all one, we are all one— think about this and apply it. When there is one or two influencers telling people their opinions, that is fine, they have free will to tell you their opinions, however, at least they should be backing this information up in sessions that you can hear. Otherwise you know that this is their Mr. Stupid mansplaining to you their opinions. All information should be heard in sessions in a raw format, as the sessions truly speak for themselves. You have more tools to reach each other than I did. The connections with communities, with the internet, should be great to grow this work and information quickly. You also know the power and significance of asking the right questions. Have your own sessions, and ask everything that is suddenly sparking in your minds now.

You know Gaia is not Earth because Earth is the name of the physical body of this planet. You know you are advanced souls who are just merely having human bodies at this moment in your play of being human. You are not the body, just as Gaia is not her body. Therefore, when you are asking about Gaia, understand what you're asking and check all labeling. Know that the soul energy frequency of the Earth is Gaia, the soul of Earth. There is a difference between asking about the body versus the soul, therefore, exploring all about the Earth experience will be enlightening.

It's complicated, but you must be aware, and listen to your own questions. Watch for any labels or names which have assumptions. Double checking with the Subconscious will always be helpful. Many are making mistakes by assuming they know what they are talking about using their human mindsets. You must be aware, and you must listen to your own questions to be able to make sure that you are actually asking the right questions. Then listen to the answers carefully— again jumping to conclusions can limit your knowledge and your clients' experiences. Keep exploring with the information. Do not be afraid to ask questions— all questions are valid, but applying the information as they are explaining it will be helpful for you. Be open minded— that is key. They are here to help you. Do not be afraid to be humble with your human mindset and admit you are not aware of all that they do. They are aware of this, however, some practitioners seem like they are not aware of that themselves.

This is a free will planet, and while all collectives and your guides want to give you all the information that they know you should get and receive and apply— if you do not use your free will to ask them the information, they cannot give it to you because that would be a breach of free will. That would be breaking the rule of non-interference. There have been many who realize this and who are using their free will to be able to get more information to be able to empower many people. Of course, when many people have got this new empowerment, it's up to them to not use their free will to discard it. That is again frustrating because they are looping to not empower themselves or not trust that many people have heard the information about the shift to New Earth. And many people have heard different collectives saying that the New Earth shift is a mindset shift, and I am saying to you that that's a small part of it, but if you read my books, you know what the information was in terms of the incarnation of Gaia. Every physical body has a birth and a death, and this goes for planets as well. As unfortunate as it is, Earth was supposed to evolve along with Gaia's soul into the fifth dimension. However, you would have to be pretty stubborn or pretty blindly ignorant to not notice the condition of your planet. You may not be aware of the energy frequency of what Gaia was going through, and if you did connect with her last year[8]— you would have felt her tremendously challenged, tortured soul struggling to keep high frequency, when she was so entrapped and encased within the intense density that was on her Earth

---

[8] Before May 2021

body. There is a saying, 'death by a thousand cuts'. It's not a gigantic loss of limb that was the cause of the death, rather it is small cuts all over the body that goes into shock, versus anything else. The planet has suffered much like this, not just physically, but energetically.

We want you to explore all of these questions. We want you to ask about everything, but we want to make sure that you have been able to get your clients into a deeper state of relaxation first. Some of you are so scared of this information, you're holding yourself and your consciousness so tight and to the surface. You really need to know the difference between your conscious mind and your connections with your Subconscious, as many of you are not getting deep enough because you're so terrified of the information, and so, therefore, are you not giving yourself the true service of this work. You can talk to yourself all day long with Mr. Stupid in charge, but the whole purpose and significance of doing these sessions is that you push your egos aside and are able to connect with advanced beings who have the sight and wisdom and knowledge of the Earth experience, because there is no such thing as time. We're able to see the full totality of the Earth's experience, and while people don't understand the concepts of time, it's all happening currently now— both your past and future have already happened, and you know this with your consciousness, if you are able to acknowledge and trust your inner knowing. That is why you are still able, just as we are still able, to tap into any day, events for any lifetime you have ever lived. Any day, any event, not just for your past experiences from this lifetime— and as practitioners you should have noticed this.

This is how we can also view other lifetimes as your guides and multi-dimensional versions of you. Since we are all one, we have access to information for all. You simply need to ask the questions to get the answers. This is all open access information. This is why you're impacted by other lifetimes today because it's all still occurring. You must be able to have some basic foundational information about how these sessions work, and how it all unfolds, and how it's all deeply connected. When you just do a course, that doesn't really give you the complete skill set. You grow along with the work. There is basic knowledge needed to understand what you're doing. It's kind of like saying, you buy a car, so therefore, you think that should instantly give you full knowledge and understand all of the engine parts and how it all works. We see many of you just hop into the driver's seats, hold on to the wheel tight, and go for it, and speed off, and that is good. You will learn. Doing these courses, you will learn when things break down or you don't get the information or the concepts you're seeking, because you are taking shortcuts either with your own inner work or you're not knowing how to deeply get and gain the trust of your clients to be able to get them to deeply relax and to be able to channel deeply for themselves.

There is much to be said here. This is not a novelty effect. These sessions are not for entertainment. These are advanced beings using this window to connect in with you to give you the support and advice and wisdom that you are privileged to be able to get because this is your birthright to be able to help humanity with. There have been so many times that humanity hasn't been profoundly helped because of their choice of free will, and their dismissal to grow and empower themselves and have faith and trust of love and respect for others. You could see the predicament that humanity has found itself in.

So I encourage and inspire you all. You're more than welcome to reach out to me, if you would rather talk to me than your own Subconscious, by simply asking me to come into the session. I will honor all who have the right intentions with this work and will do so. I still love to support and help anyway I can, but remember we're all one, and remember that it's not just the soul frequency energy you still call Dolores that has got humanity's best interests at heart. Please remember there are more here supporting you in our dimensions than actual human beings on Earth now. We outnumber you, and from our perspective of wisdom and knowledge, we're able to, we don't want to say outsmart you, because that would trigger many people who are not comfortable not knowing everything, and so we don't want to trigger you, but we want to inspire you to know the tools of how powerful and profound these sessions are.

You're very capable of reaching advanced information, but you must face fears. You must be open to all information, and you must ask hard questions and be ready to be emotionally neutral and balanced when you hear the answers. It's a journey, but what you are able to master and achieve with grace and joy is your inner peace.

In terms of learning how to be a practitioner, it is like how you can learn to drive. You can buy a course. Like how you can buy a car is easy, both can be done online. And learning how to drive is also easy with learning curves. When you start learning anything new, it can feel complicated, but also easy at the same time, so there's learning curves for all of this. It's easy to learn the script. It's easy to know how to support clients. You just have to deeply listen to them, but I am saying, just like with driving a car, you kind of need to keep the maintenance up and not have any lazy routines that start getting in the way and taking shortcuts. Remember back when you were learning, and you were very diligent and focused? Both hands were on the wheel, looking at the side mirrors, looking at the rear view mirror regularly, not over speeding, being very cautious, very aware of thinking about speed differences and speed in general, making sure that your vehicle is well maintained[9], always

---

[9] This channeler is often given analogies to give other reference points to help understand their message. This one is amusing, as the reference for channeling through a client is also referred to as

the SHIFT to NEW EARTH

having your seat belt on and so forth, and you would be washing the car regularly and that being a pride and joy. That is fantastic, and this is just a little story I want to share with you, so you can understand what I'm trying to say. When everything's new and novelty, you practice cleaning and having a good routine and maintenance, and then you get comfortable— you haven't had very many accidents. All is well, and then you start using one hand, you're not really checking your rear view mirror, you don't check your distances, and you don't check your speed, you don't check the wheels to see the tread, and you haven't changed the oil regularly; and you might even be putting some cheaper petrol into the car because of the price inflation. You also started to leave trash in the car and are not cleaning that out. And so it becomes quite run down. While you're still assuming it's going to get you from A to B, there's some bad habits, some routines that you have picked up along the way, and while this is not for everyone, this is certainly for some that I am seeing. We want you to go back to where you're learning, and be very respectful of your clients. You're listening to all that they have to share, versus telling them your thoughts and opinions of what's going on for them. These sessions aren't about you telling your clients what you think is happening with them and how they should perceive the world. For the role of the practitioners, that means you are the listener. You are

---

the vehicle, so both concepts are about how to drive the vehicle with utmost attention and respect.

gaining their trust as you are getting to know them deeply, so they can feel like they can share everything that is going on for them. This is important. Everything they're telling you is important and significant, and you mustn't dismiss any of the details. Giving them your opinions on anything they are sharing at this early point in the interview can impact your relationship. This is all valuable information they are sharing for you to do your job, so therefore, if you're trying to give them the answers to the solutions, you're missing the point of the interview process. So when you're telling them the answers— they are not feeling listened to or heard, and while they may be even grateful for your opinions— this is not what they're here for. The session is for them to share everything that is happening to them, what their concerns or worries are, where their thoughts are, and for you to gain their trust, so they can relax deeply and surrender into something that is very natural and easy, but yet feels like they are making it up. It is important for them to channel their own answers, even if you did know the same answers. They need to learn this through channeling their own guides. This is the path for true empowerment of self— giving them answers could be disempowering them, as they could think they are just repeating what they just heard from you. The practitioner should be focused on full empowerment for the client.

The client can worry it is not working for them because they have assumptions that they should not be able to recall that they're speaking or should be asleep during the process. They might feel uncomfortable that they are aware they are just sharing what pops into their minds when asked a question and can then assume this is their own thoughts. You must be able to understand this work so much from a client's point of view that you can deeply support your clients. Some of the practitioners I see have never been able to surrender in themselves to actually understand how these sessions work, to be the clients or refuse to be a regular client themselves. This is their inner work being limited here. This is a missed opportunity because the more you do sessions for yourself, not only do you heal yourself and profoundly understand yourself more, you can actually support your clients when you see that they're struggling to relax and let go. You need to understand to just accept that these subtle thoughts and senses are populated to the mind, and this is what they need to translate. This is them channeling, and it's normal and fine. With more practice it becomes more and more natural, and they can get deeper and deeper into that relaxed state of body, and therefore, brain wave. It's important for them to get their inner work explored, whatever that may be— their personal big challenges covered before you're trying to push, expose and discover the secrets of the universe. Therefore, you must be respectful, and not assume that even if they tell you how advanced they think they are, you will still need to find a way to ask the Subconscious if there is anything impacting and limiting their journey. Because otherwise, you could be missing a significant opportunity for you to be able to explore and help your clients. Everyone has inner work to work through. Make sure you have explored it while you have the chance to talk with the Subconscious. You are there for the clients to make sure that they have full empowerment, so that they can see their life with full significance and understand the purpose.

It is always best to revisit your original purpose and why you were interested in doing this work as a practitioner. Was it to help empower humanity while also helping to empower yourselves? Some of you, we see, have given up trying to understand how to make your vehicle work, to make your clients' vehicles work, to make these humans work, as you have not had so much luck or joy trying to get people to relax and be able to go into other lifetimes. Remembering there is this challenge with volunteers as they have no other lifetimes to reference upon and so you must then ask and recommend them to go to an important day in this lifetime they're living now versus trying to assume they have other lifetimes as reference points. Also understanding that some of those can be imprinted lifetimes. Therefore, your questions are very significant. Regardless of whether a soul has had that personal experience living that physical life themselves or whether it was an imprint, just simply laid upon their Earth experiences in preparation to be able to have the right skill sets and the right preferences to be able to be of service the best way they can, it is all significant.

Remember what the client's mindsets will do to themselves, in terms of creating illnesses or blocks in mental expansions. This is all about what's going on for them, if they are focused and fixated and judging, if there is any imbalance, whether they are angry or whether they are hurt. They will show you and tell you what they can't love. Usually it is they can't love themselves from a standpoint. When they can't love themselves, they are seeking love from others. This is very draining, and they can find it very unfulfilling to not feel the love of others. They have this expectation that humans can love them like Source love energy, like God love energy, whatever you want to call it. It may be hard for them to experience parents and the lack of the love that they were expecting as a child. Humans are always going to be humans, and they'll always have limitations of being able to provide each other with love. Children are going to struggle when they are not surrounded in Source love energy growing up, and that is significant. That is to teach them to balance and empower themselves, and to make them understand right from the get-go, the game of life, of being human, and the limitations of energy frequency that they feel. The more you understand what truly are the principles and purposes and the typical experiences of the limitations of being here on Earth for a soul, the easier you will find being here now.

We understand that when you are trained to think that you should only focus on positive, and only think about positive things, that that will keep you high frequency vibrations, and that is not how you get there— you must be honest and see everything as it truly is, without letting that completely destroy your moral compasses and your emotional well-being. This is why this is important work to explore and understand and ask the significance and the purposes of everything.

An empath is going to be more drawn to doing this work because they deeply care and support and love humanity on an intensively, compassionate level. And yet when they can feel the pain of everyone, this will make them retreat and not want to hear and face the facts, that this is a hard and challenging life. There is beautiful purpose and significance in all of this, but when you cannot understand the lessons involved with hunger, homelessness, with diseases, with illnesses, with disabilities in general, when you are scared of dying, you forget to live fully and completely. These are all fascinating topics for you to explore as a practitioner. It is significant, and if you are not finding true inner peace and balance and joy within yourself and accept everything that's happening on this Earth as it truly is— all of the agendas that are trying to disempower humanity, distract humanity from its spiritual journey of growth to remember collectively you're all one— this is a significant lesson for you to remind yourselves. You must be thinking about regular hygiene in terms of your spiritual growth and go regularly to have your own sessions to see if there is anything that you have as a belief system that is out of date, or that needs to be explored upon and expanded upon. Don't be afraid of learning new information, knowledge and wisdom. Embrace it and feel excited about it, because the more questions and answers you receive— the better you can keep your balance and neutrality. This is a fundamental key to being a fantastically wonderful practitioner, and this is why it is recommended that you work together as a team and give each other sessions. The more sessions you have, the better you will be able to support humanity, and ultimately, you're all here to support humanity. Be brave with your questions, honor all feelings, respect all, and go with love and peace and joy. The true value of inner peace is **wisdom**, and when you know and understand you are always protected, you're always guided, and this is one of many experiences that you will have— you can have balance and not take this life so seriously. Because you're all so hyper-focused on your personal insecurities or egos— that you're kind of missing the point and principles of living. Get going and explore it, question everything, and see how you too can gain higher advantage points of perspectives that help assist you with your wisdom and journey, and I say this with love.

Session 1

J: How is her body going?

S: Well, very well.

J: Fantastic, thank you, and so can you remind me, please, Subconscious, what dimension are you in?

S: In the 9th.

J: Thank you so much, and from your perspective, in terms of the "shift", what does shifting to 5D mean for humanity?

S: There's so many meanings. We are releasing what we are holding on to, which is these carbon-based bodies, into our crystalline forms, moving to a new planet. This planet, Earth, can no longer sustain life much longer, and all are aware of that subconsciously. All animals. All plants. All humans. No one is forgotten.

J: Thank you, and what is the life contract for this planet's soul, in terms of shifting to the fifth dimension?

S: We see she is gonna be a beautiful new planet. She's excited, and she has been waiting for this. She's been suffering for a long time here on Earth, but she's been released, and we are preparing her to step into that new role as the New Earth soul for that planet.

J: Thank you, thank you so much, and so what is the term Old Earth referring to?

S: We foresee it and always felt the most appropriate beginning of Old Earth would be directly after the laser event occurs.

J: Okay, thank you, and so then from your perspective, what could be the life lessons for those people experiencing the Old Earth?

S: There can be many. It could be to learn trust and faith in oneself, one's abilities. Compassion towards others. Finishing out any kind of life contracts with others. So if somebody serviced you in some way, in another lifetime, for example, and you still never were able to service them, it's like bringing it all together. You're just finishing everything, everyone's finishing everything. Everything needs to be tied up and completed, and so any unfinished business, we could say, any unfinished situations, are to be done now. It's a lot of working with other people. If the person has not done well on that or avoided people all their lives, being forced into situations where you're forced to work with others to survive. Many things humbling others. People who have got everything that they felt like they wanted materialistically, having things taken away, learning to appreciate what little they have left. It depends.

J: Thank you, yes, I do know that these are such broad questions, but I really do appreciate the confirmation that once again you're providing for us. What is New Earth?

S: New Earth is a new planet, a 5D planet. No physicalness, there, it's all energy, it's all frequency, it's all high vibrational, so we don't foresee things as being necessarily how it'd be here. It's not dense where things are solid in their form; they're quite malleable there. They do not want people with any type of density on there. You have to be at the same frequency. You have to be able to get to the same frequency; readjust yourself beforehand. Those who are going to the New Earth will go there, and we want to say it's pretty much now decided. It's like they're trying to give people chances, but it's becoming so small now because time's running out. They're doing the last minute things, and if they choose not to step into that, and decide to go elsewhere, that is okay too.

J: Absolutely, thank you, and so can you tell me the main differences between the carbon-based bodies and the crystalline-based bodies? I'm assuming you're trying to say to me that one's in 3D and one's in 5D?

S: You cannot take this body out of 3D, it is not possible. You're not light enough. Your soul doesn't want to be tethered to this. This is heavy, this isn't fun for the soul. The soul finds it to be very burdensome, almost like a heavy suit. They want to be free, and the crystalline body is much lighter. It's all energy, and we've seen it before with its beautiful colors, all different colors. However, we know that when you go into the 5D, we feel like you have the opportunity to change into pretty much any kind of look you want. It does not matter look wise, but with the crystalline bodies, it's something that can be in the 5D frequency on that planet.

J: Thank you so much. We're hearing from many other people talking about the New Earth being here now on this planet and that we are in the fifth dimension. Where are they getting that information from?

S: Their teams are actually prompting them with information, and it's so they won't be in density, and it's giving them this hopium, this hope that there is something great, and it's 5D. It's like they're giving them the messages, and they're believing that it's happening here because they wouldn't be able to cope with the reality of it, of all the intricacies of it. Some souls just aren't ready to hear that. Some are based here on Earth, and they have not had that ability to open their mindsets that far out. So it's helping those with more simplistic, more grounded into the Earth type of personalities, to assist them with the possibilities of 5D. It's doing a good job, as it's keeping their vibrations higher because they have hope and belief.

J: I love that, and so in terms of people being activated or learning this information, can you give me a sense of how many people are still seeking this truth, this level of truth?

S: This level of truth is definitely something people need to step up towards because they will not hear the messages. Are you asking how many are still seeking this truth right now, how many percent?

J: Yes, how many people will be awoken by these future sessions that we can provide?

S: We're getting like 75 percent. There's a trickling effect, so as people are listening to these sessions, there's a trickling out where their mindsets expand and energy does not die. It only changes. So it goes out and out and out and when you open your mindsets to certain things, you start to reach frequencies that start to open yourself up to higher frequency communication; which in turn almost becomes magnetized around those people who are around you. The density starts lifting as you start raising your vibrations up and your intuition, your clarity, and those around you also will get the same effect, maybe not as quickly, but somewhat.

J: So those people who are saying that the New Earth or the 5D is just a mindset; that's just one step truly towards the actual shifting to the New Earth?

S: Correct. Those who are very much into this grounding on the Earth, you see them almost like they're newer, they're not old, they just haven't had the opportunity yet to be that advanced in their minds, and so they're newer to information, and that would be too fast.

J: I understand. It does seem consistent that a lot of the volunteers who are here on this Earth have found this information sort of primarily, before, or over, shall I say, the newer souls.

S: Correct, the newer souls do not look at this Earth, like it just is what it is, and it is hard for them to imagine other possibilities or the intricacies. It would actually make them shut down. It would be too much.

J: Very true, okay, thank you. Do you feel like there are any more questions I should be asking in this series of ten different clients? I'm having these same questions or some very similar questions given to their Subconscious?

S: We're getting a sense that it might be helpful to ask them about New Earth. Ask them what happens when you arrive on New Earth? What does it look like? We almost want you to ask them to take a peek.

J: Ok, take a peek at New Earth, that sounds fantastic. And so, when we ask this vehicle to take a peek on New Earth, what does she notice?

S: The meadow, that is her place she likes to run back and forth. She's had plays there for quite a while because she's over there for a while.

J: Running!![10]

S: It's not running but it's like running, yes. There she has no legs, she has no feet.

J: I get it, you can take the body off of that girl, but you can't take the running out of that girl! That's cool, okay, I can respect that. Is there anything else that she can see when she is peeking around the New Earth and exploring? What else does she notice?

S: She's mentioned this before, but it makes her happy that the animals are also able to speak, and you're also able to form really strong friendships and relationships with the animals. So everything is communicative.

J: Yes, very strong connections to all, and I guess that's probably the reason why there can't be any being there with low density because that high frequency of everyone needs to be maintained to expand upon. Because after the fifth dimension, is the primary step forward, after that would be the seventh dimension? Is that correct or something else?

---

[10] After over a dozen sessions together this is a long running joke that she loves to run.

S: We do not see it as that. People can go to other 5D planets, and so it's dependent upon what they choose. They can explore. Of course, those who would like to get to the seventh can, depending upon what they choose to do, and what they want to accomplish. We foresee a lot of exploring in the fifth dimension because it is so fun.

J: Did you have many lifetimes in the fifth dimension yourself, Subconscious?

S: Plenty, plenty.

J: Okay, well, we won't pry. Are there any other questions that you think would be valid on this little series that I'm planning to do with other people asking them the same similar questions?

S: Let's see, other questions, well those are all just little intricacies. We see everything as it should be. They are valid questions. We do find it to be enjoyable for each person to see the New Earth, which is why we would like that to be prompted, and it gives them that excitement.

J: Thank you, so once we get excited, we have quite strong empowerment and inspiration to be able to share this information and help others to love themselves and to stop their addiction of density.

S: Yes, and now there's much more ahead. It's difficult sometimes in 3D.

J: When people listen to this small portion of this session, will they have any questions or challenges to overcome or understand? What would you like me to know about how people will respond and process this information that has been delivered through this vehicle?

S: They will enjoy it. They will appreciate it. Those who listen to these sessions are very connected with their teams, very connected with themselves; been on this journey and they know themselves, they know much. We do not foresee any shock. They will be more grateful for the information.

J: I love that. Okay, well, I'm so grateful, so thank you very much, Subconscious, for all the divine information you've given us today. We really appreciate it. Are there any further messages for the vehicle or myself?

S: We feel great peace. We really enjoyed this transmission. We thank you both.

J: Wonderful, thank you so much. We really appreciate hearing so many fantastic things from you, to inspire us and to have empowerment and encouragement. How is her body? How is she going to feel after the session because we want her to feel fantastic and energized and a real big powerhouse for her future events?

S: She feels much better now and we will continue working with her. Her whole body feels good.

J: Okay, well, thank you so much[11].

---

[11] The epiphany to do this series of sessions was given, and then this session was the first to explore this. This is only part of that session. As you can see, we ask our guides about this, and they have been a big part of this series to make sure we are supporting humanity the best way we can. With love for you all. We sincerely hope this inspires you.

the SHIFT to NEW EARTH

Session 2

J: We are here, we are here, we are here, and we say this with somewhat humor because it was us truly that have prompted these series sessions. We are happy to be able to assist with something we have prompted the vehicle to be able to organize and orchestrate.

S: Well, thank you. We do appreciate it. Subconscious, can we do a body scan, please, for the vehicle?

J: Yes, she is in true balance and harmony. She has been for so long. But she always wants to put a little bit too much pressure on herself, and that is her choosing. She uses her free will sometimes interestingly, but we often give her so much healing, and as she's working in this state and energy frequently, she really has nothing to complain about.

S: Fantastic, how's the body feeling right now?

J: We will say she feels like champagne on a beautiful beach.

S: Sounds lovely, that's great.

J: The vehicle is saying that's not. She doesn't have the taste for champagne, so she doesn't get the reference, but that is fine. We'll relax the mind and speak with you directly, as we are pushing aside her worries and concerns about what champagne tastes like.

S: Thank you, thank you, Subconscious. We do have some questions today, and we're wondering if you can assist us with this?

J: Yes, indeed, you do, and yes, indeed, we can.

S: Okay, thank you. Subconscious, which dimension are you currently residing in?

J: There are many of us, and we are speaking to you from the ninth dimension, however, we have got assistances to be able to support this conversation today with much higher collectives who are watching us, as we are watching you.

S: What are the highest dimensions that are assisting today? Just curious.

J: We see that there are members that are already within the Source collective, and so we dropped the labels. As we drop our bodies and our essences become souls, true forms of souls when we become true Source. There are many aspects and essences. We're wanting to remind the vehicle that when you start getting fixated on dimensions and where one resides, you can almost become limited.

S: Okay, is there anything else you'd like us to know about that?

J: Well, we could tell you that the vehicle is listening and saying she gets our point. She then is wondering if she's making mistakes with her assumptions that she needs to label and define so many things, such as dimensions, but we are with much love reminding her that there are so many aspects to all that she is curious about. And to just have open-mindedness as you are learning, while you may need to learn to have focus and use labels, that is fine. But know when you have outgrown the labels that helped assist you with your fundamental and foundational understanding of what she calls— the metaphysics.

S: Thank you very much. Thank you for that. Subconscious, our next question is from your perspective in terms of the "shift." What does shifting to 5D mean for humanity?

J: Yes, it means that on a collection of many days and many events, humans will be shifting from this dimension to another dimension. This will be done all together but not at the same split moment in time as you perceive time. So humanity will be shifting from what you are currently residing at, which is in the third dimension, and you will be gaining much more higher perspective and mindsets and in physicality as your bodies evolve swiftly, graciously and with ease.

S: Thank you, is there anything else you'd like to share with us about that?

J: This is a term that has been bastardized by many, as they have lazily assumed that the shifting is just merely a state of mind, a state of consciousness, and we say, where is the rest? Why are you not able to, with your spiritual egos, broaden your horizons, broaden your expansion of information? This must trigger so many, when you are so scared to see the bigger truth right in front of you. We're not trying to offend, but it is not time to play small, quaint games of mindsets and only being mindsets. It's all around you. It's obvious what your bodies are doing, what your planet has been doing, and why you're so focused on labels and terms and following fake, limited influencers. You've not noticed the current situation that your planet is in. It's all around you, and yet, you choose to distract yourselves with celebrities, fake wars, destruction, hatred upon each other, and judgment. We see this. While we do not judge you, we wonder how on Earth could humanity feel so comfortable and proud of itself when the majority are so fixated on such limited dense perspectives? But that is part of the experience. While it's not our cup of tea, shall we say, it clearly is many beings' cups of tea, as they love that density, love the dramas. Some of us view that as very tiresome, but for some, they love the challenges and exploring. It's almost like they would never have enough. They've always got a thirst and a quench for the dynamics of the physical realms, and for some of us, we couldn't imagine anything almost as worse. But that is our choice, so please respect us. We're not trying to judge you. We know many of you have come down there to be able to be of service and assistance and we applaud you. We applaud you because you are such advanced souls, and it's so tiresome when you feel like you're trying to encourage and cheerlead and help assist humanity, while humanity is tuning you out, not listening to you, not respecting you and looking at new gossip and distractions and focusing more on that than their own spiritual growth, their own spiritual evolution, their own family and friends.

S: Thank you, for the next question, Subconscious, I would like to ask: what is the term "Old Earth" referring to? Is this still a future event humanity will experience?

J: Indeed, as we said before, you will not shift all in the same one split second, in its progressing stages. You must see for your own eyes: the decline, the health decline, the physicality decline of the planet. Once you start seeing it break down, it's starting to decay. What you would not perceive as decay, you would just assume is a mini series of unfortunate events. However, when you have to start seeing and living and noticing this rapid change, you'll start being more aware of your surroundings, less focused on your phones, more focused on surviving. The Old Earth is the decline of the physicality of the body of this planet you are residing on in your physical bodies.

S: Yes, thank you, is there anything else you'd like to add with that?

J: As you know, with any physical death of a body, it does decay, and so for us to explain to you all of the nuances of every part of the body that starts collapsing, and without the energy supporting it, as we start focusing more on the evacuation of this planet. You will notice things rapidly declining, but it is like saying, "You're watching a dead body, what are the most significant things you would want to notice about it?" When you're looking at the entire body, we could talk about all the nuances and all the locations and how they're going to experience things, so when we try to talk to you, we know all of this, but we're trying to give you the most appropriate information for you to brace yourself emotionally, trusting all is well. All is purposeful. You've asked for these experiences to be able to help assist humanity at this time, and you'll do it well.

S: Thank you, Subconscious, is there going to be any type of event right before the Old Earth or an event that will start the Old Earth?

J: As we were referring to, there are many events that will be occurring, but when you are on the official Old Earth? You are already currently on the official Old

Earth. You're on Earth, and it is old. When would you like to start your labeling and your branding of your experience? Many of you will need such bigger events to occur for you to be able to think, 'right, this must be the moment,' and so it will be obvious for many and subtle for others because they won't be in the direct location of certain events. You may not be in the path of the destruction, and so you may just hear it on the news or something else. Each individual being will have a different experience of what is happening because you're in different locations around the world. It is going to be a more challenging, focused way of life, and as this may shock you to hear, some people actually flourish and thrive on the survival experience because it takes them out of their mundane routine. There is so much to be said, but as you may have heard, prepare for everything because potentially everything must unfold and incur for people to notice and accept the state of your planet

S: Thank you, is there anything else you'd like us to know about that?

J: It was a shortened Earth experience. We did plan and have great hopes that this planet's survival rate could have been much longer. We say this for the soul of the planet and not so much for the souls and the experiences of those who are on this planet. You are merely visitors to her, and we see the greatest soul, which you call Gaia. We have been supporting her life experience, her life contract, and while you're having your merely fleeting multiple lifetimes on this beautiful vessel that you call Earth, nothing could have prepared us for the behaviors and the use of free will that took upon this planet, that drained her of her life forces in the third dimension. As you are aware, she had planned to do such marvelous things, and she will be able to do that. She will always be granted... (J gasps in emotional pain.) The vehicle was having a reaction to the emotions. The reaction was this when we were saying to you that the soul of this planet will always be granted her life contracts and wishes. As she wants to experience certain things, such as being planets, she'll always be granted approval and permission to be able to obtain a new planet to be able to evolve from the third to the fifth dimensions. The reason why the vehicle got the extreme overwhelming feeling is our love for Gaia, and so she's having a physical reaction to it. We will relax her into it. Please continue with your questions.

S: Okay, thank you for helping her relax. We just ask for as much relaxation as possible, and how is her body doing right now?

J: Her body is very well, it is very balanced and in harmony. It is her emotions that will get her into trouble.

S: Love is a very strong emotion.

J: Our love for your planet soul was tremendous and profound because she has been of great service, not just this lifetime as being Gaia, but she is so precious, like you were all so precious. As you can imagine, we have seen so much tragedy happen to her. Much hardship, and while it was done to her, her free will was taken from her in some regards because she had her life contract cut short, in this third dimension. While she is completely fine and marvelous, and while we could say she is that champagne on the most beautiful beach in the world herself, living her best fabulous life, we are still so dismayed by people's choices, humanity's choices to be so neglectful in considering others, including this beautiful soul that you call Gaia.

S: Yes, a really great reminder. This actually was answered in a way, however, I would still like to ask the question: what is the life contract for this planet's soul in terms of shifting to 5D?

J: Originally it was to be able to evolve naturally and beautifully here on this planet and to be able to advance herself energetically into the fifth dimension. It was going to be brilliant, and as we discussed, this has changed, and so she is now able to simply slip into a new higher frequency planet where she will be able to enjoy having her fifth dimensional experience that way. We see that while she enjoys all of that lifetime, she will love being that new planet, that New Earth, within that soul of that New Earth. We see that she could potentially have a walkout experience, when she is ready to then go into a new third-dimensional planet, and then be able to have

the SHIFT to NEW EARTH

her complete cycle that way, where she experiences a more in balance, in harmony with a third dimensional life as a physical planet. Then she wants to graduate and evolve into a fifth dimension and explore that physicality. Evolving her body that way, she wants to be able to raise her frequency naturally so much that she transmutes instantly over time. It must sound like such a contradiction because it will be a gradual thing, when she finally gets to experience her whole desire to be able to shift from the third to the fifth— and one physical body and not have to reincarnate as she has to at this point. So it has changed, and we have supported her along the way. It's so rich in extra experiences, and while we're grateful for the experiences, some of us are still seeing, this is all so unnecessary because the trauma that impacts souls can be so great. While we have perceptions, as we're looking down or sideways or above or below, however, you want to perceive our dimension where we are now. We still have an opinion that this was still so unnecessary. We can admit that we still have to see how it all unfolds and affects timelines and experiences, to be able to see how it all unfolds ourselves. We are still so busy focusing on this project now that we haven't had a moment to stop and look at the full totality of what these lessons and experiences eventuate to. We will just pause and expand upon this concept because we're so in the moment of discussing the sadness and the challenges of this planet. While we can see that the soul is completely fine, being on holiday on a beautiful beach, which is just her temporary spot, it's not a beach, and she isn't truly champagne, but she's doing so well. She is doing so well. We can see all the perspectives. We just indulge ourselves and think about all that went 'wrong' for her to not be able to shift into the fifth dimension here on your planet that you're on now. We've taken a distraction. We're focused on a point so much that we even forgot for ourselves that we know the outcome was fantastic. We know that all is well, and we know that all is purposeful, and we can see the profound effects that have rippled out through the universe. Why did we focus so suddenly on what had gone wrong? Because in the broader scheme of things all is perfect, all is well. Everything is balanced. All is harmony, but you must be able to see the full totality of it all, and not look at the details. So pardon us for focusing on the challenges.

S: That is quite understandable. Thank you, though, for the information, and is there anything else you'd like to add to that?

J: We're still learning how to be able to support those who want less challenging 3D lifetimes to be able to evolve into the fifth dimension along with soul and body.

S: Is there any other information you'd like to share with us with regards to Gaia and her life contract?

J: She is going well; it has changed. It has been updated. All is well. Gaia will still get an opportunity to have her original contract honored. It will not be on this planet, this physical planet, and also will not be on the New Earth[12] because it's already advanced itself into the fifth dimension. She will be honored and gifted another new body. Potentially we see that she walks out of the New Earth soul as another soul wants to practice being a fifth dimensional soul essence of a planet. Gaia is then merged into a beautiful new planet for her to be able to complete this. All life contracts are respected. This is an especially respected life contract for her to have.

S: Thank you, thank you again for the clarification. Subconscious, with the next question, could you explain to us what could be some life lessons for people experiencing the Old Earth?

J: Realizations— that they are surrounded themselves, and they're living on a dying planet. So they will have to wake up to where they are and their environment. They have been ignoring it while they have been distracting themselves with many things. They have to be responsible, and then suddenly take accountability to what they're living on and how they have been treating this. Well, of course, they won't often actually feel apart and responsible for the decline of this planet. They will be having to experience the consequences of such while they're thinking it's natural. Some of those who are living

---

[12] Gaia will have another 3D body after her New Earth experience, where all will merge into the 5D with that one — from recent sessions we have explored about this.

on this planet are quite responsible for making certain choices and decisions in other lifetimes to impact this planet, and potentially other planets with not great intentions for all, including the soul of the planets.

S: Is there anything else you'd like us to know about that?

J: Yes, consequences. Having to live out consequences is what you could call karma, but they need to have these epiphanies and experiences to realize that while you may have gotten away with certain behaviors in other lifetimes, you cannot escape being responsible— having to be responsible for certain events. While it must feel mean and sad, these people, these beings, have wanted to experience being accountable for the destruction of a planet, and being accountable for mis-guiding and misleading humanity and other species. Again, it's not a punishment because you've all chosen to be here. You all want to have these experiences. It's all for the commonality of the collectives to be able to learn and grow from it, to heal from it. There's so many important experiences to be had on the Old Earth. It's all highly significant.

S: Totally agree with lots of lessons, much growth as well. Thank you. Thank you for sharing that. Subconscious, could you please tell us what New Earth is?

J: It is a new planet. It has been designed to be set at the frequency of the fifth dimension, so the vibration is quite high. If you tried to take your physical bodies now onto that planet, it would be like what the vehicle would assume is putting a fly in a microwave, and you would explode. You cannot hold the frequency of that. She doesn't understand how microwaves work, so this may not be the most appropriate analogy to share with you all. If we put your physical bodies in 3D onto the New Earth, it would not look good. You would turn into very dense matter. You'd almost implode. We're showing her this difference, and it's not pleasant. We have fumbled into a detailed distraction as we are showing her. The question was about the New Earth, and what is the New Earth, and our response is: it's a new planet designed for the soul of your current planet you're living on now. The New Earth is her reincarnation body into the fifth dimension— what she will slip into. She will be able to have an enjoyable fifth dimensional experience as being a planet. You can imagine the new planet in a fifth dimension density has got lots of advancements for you to explore. Did we answer your question sufficiently?

S: Yes, thank you. So, Subconscious, are you trying to say that we cannot bring our carbon-based bodies to the New Earth?

J: Not as you are in your physical body right now. You could take the illusion of who you are right now with you, with your soul essence, to the New Earth, as you perceive yourself. You would be projecting an illusion of your physical, carbon-based body that you're living in now, but it wouldn't be the same. It's very different. You wouldn't be physically solid. You would be translucent, but we want to say this for humor because the vehicle was feeling a little bit dense with exploring some of the content about the sadness of where this planet has gone, and how it was so unnecessary. We're going to say this for humor, so please do not take us literally. People who hold on to the illusion of their carbon-based bodies are like that old man who does comb overs with their hair, thinking he still looks good. You know he doesn't have hair all over his head. You know he is balding. He knows he's balding, but he tries to have the illusion that he's got a full head of hair. Therefore, it is like for people who are trying to keep the illusion of their physical 3D bodies on their soul essence to project out to those on the New Earth. At some point you all know and accept you're not fooling anyone. There is no need to do the comb overs, and there is no need to keep projecting a human looking carbon body on the New Earth. You just have to let go of your insecurities. You are soul essences with crystalline bodies. You are not needing to have a veneer, but that is just merely a projection of an illusion, that you have a physical body[13]. When you get more comfortable being there, you won't need it. We are sorry that we have tried to make the vehicle have humor. She doesn't judge people and their hair, but we thought that this would be a funny statement to say. Her heart feels so heavy

---

[13] In the session they used the word which sounded like a "layment" — like an overlay of the physical looking body over the soul. Because there was a stumble over a word that was edited out.

because she went deep into seeing what Gaia had to experience. She also was experiencing the density of Old Earth, and so for you to ask about the New Earth, we wanted to uplift her and bring humor back into her energy field.

S: Is there any way we can assist her with releasing the density during the session?

J: She is judging us for our lame dad joke. [Laughter] All is well, all is well. We will give her a sneak peak of the New Earth, and she instantly wants to cry, because she can feel the joy of Gaia. This is something that this soul essence of this vehicle has wanted for so long— to have the liberation of Gaia. Gaia is so important and loved by so many. This is the very first sense that the vehicle gets when she notices that she is on the New Earth— just the profound gratitude and gratefulness that she can sense, the happiness of Gaia. It's truly uplifting the soul. It just feels so positive, liberated. It is so beautiful. This is exactly what Gaia has always deserved. It is quite breathtaking, the energy, because it's just so pure and so liberating, with a high frequency. It is joy— beyond joy, multiplied by joy, infused with love. It is so profound. It is such a celebration for Gaia. When she does overcome the overwhelmingness of just gratitude for the soul of the planet being so free, she will be able to compose herself and feel gratitude for herself that she is also at this frequency. It is so bright. It is so vibrant. It is so alive. The vessel has now reflected and compared the planet she is living on now and is saying to us, 'my gosh, it feels so dead— this planet here now'. The vehicle was wanting to scream, 'How long have we been on Old Earth for?' Because that is her label of Old Earth time frame being this intense density[14]. It literally is this planet already. She's only known the density of this planet her entire life. She's so overwhelmed with emotions. We're focusing back, because she was experiencing that profound New Earth experience, and then she had to flip to compare the difference. Then it just suddenly dropped her into that density. It's a very stark difference. It feels like polar opposites of frequency. It's quite a tremendous difference; it's not subtle. Well, it's certainly not just a mindset. It's quite intensive.

S: Okay, yes, I totally understand. It's quite amazing, and it's quite overwhelming in the positive sense.

J: Yes, and then when you flip back into the density, you realize that you've been on the Old Earth for so long. The vehicle's[15] the entire existence of Earth has been on the

---

[14] This experience shocked me for days, I actually thought I did a primal scream out loud during this, and while it was barely a minute experience on Earth time, my journey was much longer than that. It can be common for the subconscious to tell their vessels they will not take them to New Earth in sessions, as it is hard enough to cope being here now. This would be the last straw for them, and they would want to give up living here. It is very important to be here now and to be as empowered as we can. Love is key for all, and that will help all here in 3D.

[15] The label they refer to is about the person having the session and channeling in their higher dimensional selves.

Old Earth— her entire lifetime. While the energy is trying to boost itself up, to try and get out of some of the density, it is still an extremely dense planet. This planet you're on now is incredibly so. While the density of the planet is increasing, as your physical bodies are increasing until more of a higher frequency, if you could actually tap into the energy of this planet, it's very dense. We've almost buffered you from feeling that true density of the planet. It's unavoidable. You cannot release the planet's density like this. When you're feeling those big vibes of high frequency, it's just for the beings. It cannot be provided to the planet anymore. This is something she has not realized so dramatically before. The vehicle could feel Gaia's soul essence; she couldn't distinguish between the actual planet's density and Gaia's density. Now she just had the extreme fifth dimensional experience with Gaia on the New Earth, and then she went consciously back to this current planet to feel the density, and it's beyond extreme. We are just simply relaying to you what the vehicle has been exploring and experiencing. We apologize, and we have just verbalized the reactions and responses. Please continue with the questions, and we will focus.

S: Okay, thank you for all the intriguing information. I love that you're sharing so much, and I would actually like to bring her back to the New Earth, and I would like her to explain to us what she is seeing there?

J: Yes, it's a high intensive frequency of energy. So what she sees is the correlation between that high frequency, that love, that joy, that harmony, that unity. Because you feel so fantastic in that frequency, you radiate. You try to translate that energy into beauty, into something like the most beautiful place in the world. Because you're trying to translate that high frequency into something physical, but you can't actually, truly do physical things there, so you're creating the illusion. You're transcribing, you're describing, you're transmuting how you're feeling in the fifth dimension into creating from this beautiful frequency. The joy that you feel in that frequency creates so much around you. It's like you can create music and you can physically see that music, so you have all these extra senses that are translating this beautiful energy of being in the fifth dimension. Yet, you're not physically creating certain things that you are responding to that energy, to that frequency. You're creating how that makes you feel— you're translating, you are expressing the fifth dimension throughout you and around you. You are a light being who is responding to this beautiful energy around you, and you are creating more energy, more light, more frequency. Because it's so within you, you get to see it as— we are struggling to even try to express it— you feel love within you here, but on the New Earth, when you feel love, you express it out. You see the love you feel, and the love you feel will be a beautiful meadow that you create, beautiful flowers that you create, beautiful things, and reference to be able to express how you feel within. You are translating that out

the SHIFT to NEW EARTH

in these energetic forms of flowers and gardens and oceans and so much, and you are all so connected in. You're all co-creating— your paradise, your harmony, your love, your freedom, your evolution. There's so much to share. You can't withhold any thoughts or feelings. You're not independent as such anymore because you're so deeply connected to all. When you don't have any density, when you don't have any worries, when you don't have any distractions, all you're trying to do is express beauty and love, true love, real love, and the highest almost integrity of Source love. Because you don't have any density, don't have any doubts, don't even have any worries, so you fully allow yourself to feel it all. And you're all bouncing off each other. You're radiating off each other because of the frequency of the fifth dimension of that planet. It is so impossible to fully be able to describe how you just radiate the frequency from within you out beyond yourself, from within you to beyond you. You feel it so deeply within your soul essence that you radiate out your translations of that elated joy, elated love, beyond your love frequency that you can obtain now. It really starts off so strong, and it continues to be so strong, the more you go along, the more you can create more. It is a beautiful step, and there is so much to explore. It takes practice to really transmute and adjust. You have no density, but it takes some practice to process not having that density. It's beyond beautiful, but it's nearly too hard to comprehend it with a three-dimensional density mindset.

S: So beautiful. I love that, thank you. Are there any other differences in the way we'd be living on the New Earth verses here that you'd like to share with us?

J: It's like extremes. You're so connected with each other on the New Earth. You love each other and respect each other, want to dance with each other and have joy with each other. It feels extremely different, and so it feels so joyous to be on the New Earth. Your bodies are different. Everything really is different. We understand that knowing the extreme differences does concern many people. They get so stressed— they are so worried about what they're leaving and losing that they marinate themselves even deeper into density, and it is just the most, we say this with much love, the most absurdist thing. You've had so many lifetimes in density. It is time. This planet is nearly done. You cannot continue on playing your 3D games when the soul essence of this planet has nearly all but departed. You are on, we would say, limited borrowed time, and all is well. You will be so astonished how marvelous and beautiful and connected you are all on the New Earth. You will feel so blissful. You will not even comprehend why you were so obsessed and fixated on these denser lives. It's uncomparable.

S: Thank you, Subconscious. My next question is: could you tell us the main difference between our carbon-based bodies (what we have now) versus the crystalline bodies?

J: They're very different. They still contain the soul essence, but we would say one is more physical and one is mostly physical[16]. You are very dense when you're 3D. In the 5th Dimension, you think you're physical, but you can manipulate your energy field. When you reach that comfortability, when you realize that you don't need to have a comb over anymore, shall we say, back to the analogy of the old man joke. You get to choose your clothes every day— how you want to present yourself and your light based crystalline bodies. It takes a while for you to get comfortable with not being humanoid looking bodies. You all sort of feel joyous and still want to feel normal as a human, so you still cling on to your illusions of being a physical human. For those original souls, you'll always be classed as human, regardless of where and how you evolve. It is your physical life journey. If you originally had a first physical lifetime here, this is your original, home planet Earth— where the Earth was your school for the 3D experience. This is your home planet. We know many collectives have many names for Earthlings— humans on Earth. There are many other names, but as we said from the very start, don't get caught up in labels for your descriptions because it can limit you.

---

[16] Both the carbon-based bodies and the crystalline-based bodies are physical, but carbon-based bodies are more dense. For example, water can be in physical form as both ice and mist.

S: Thank you, is there anything else you would like to add?

J: Change is inevitable, you cannot stop what is coming. Evolution is always going to be an advancement; there needs to be an evolutionary step. We will work together to make sure that this is easy, less dramatic, and evolution is always a bonus. What you may understand is that your perceived evolution here on this planet is somewhat corrupted with your history. We want to reassure any who are still scared of this evolution step for themselves. Potentially you've done this so many times. You all have your veil of forgetfulness still here on Earth. You cannot recall all the other times you've simply slipped in and out of your physical bodies as soul essences. But trust all as well.

S: Beautiful, thank you. Subconscious, we're hearing many people talking about the New Earth being here on this planet, and just wondering, where are they getting this information from?

J: Their limited egos and perspectives because they're fear-based. They know that there is a change coming, and so many people are asking about it because they're getting dreams. They're being pushed and encouraged to talk about it, but yet they don't know what they're talking about, so they jump onto labels and names with assumptions that they know what they're talking about. But, unfortunately, the New Earth is not here. You are not in the fifth dimension, and it's not even physically possible for you to be in a carbon-based body and be in the fifth dimension. It is all about physics; the most basic redundant understanding of physics spells it out to you all what a fifth dimensional object looks like versus a third. So tell us, Mr. Smartypants human, monkeys that have evolved three steps above monkeys, can we say this with love to humanity? Ultimately you are very rudimentary in your evolution steps, with your mindsets, and your brain capacity. You were only ever supposed to experience a few emotions and then find your way back to love while having a physical body, and look how complicated you've made it. You were supposed to love each other with tribes, share it with some soul family, and look how complicated it got, so far quickly off the original life purpose for Earth. We distracted ourselves with your question. Why is humanity hiding the truth about the evolutionary shift to a fifth dimensional planet? Well, humanity is still used to lying to each other. You're still so used to lying to yourselves, about your true desires, your true longing for love. There is so much to be said here. It is all stepping stones when those people are trying to tell you about the New Earth, suggesting something new is happening. You all know something is happening, you can feel it in your bones. You can feel it in your souls, you can feel it and your heart beats. You can feel the rush, you can feel it coming faster. You can feel it intensively, and you know it's coming. However, you can't take that next step and feel that you surrender into all of the processes, to then be able to get to the next emotional excitement of joy, the next emotional stage which is excitement and joy. You're still so dense, you can't even get to the next step of being excited and looking forward to what's to come because you're still so distracted with the density you're currently in. We have given you many answers. Was this enough for you to understand? Perhaps we want to say judgmental opinions, but it truly is observation of how humanity has conducted itself.

S: An honest viewpoint of observation.

J: Because so many humans are so dishonest with themselves, they react so dramatically to the truth. They gasp. They freak out in fear. They dismiss it so instantly when the truth is given directly to their faces, to their ears, to their souls. You cannot lie to your soul.

S: That is very true, yes, beautifully said. Subconscious, is there anything else you'd like to add with that specific topic?

J: Do not be afraid to connect with all. You will stop lying to each other, you'll stop despising each other, you'll stop hating each other. You'll stop fearing each other. What you will be doing on the New Earth with each other is love. Love is all things. Love is all there is, and love is all you need. When you are able to have that profound connection to love of self and to love of all, that is the frequency that you're all yearning for. You all deserve this. We say for those souls who have been patiently waiting to assist, to reassure them — not much longer now.

S: Thank you so much, thank you. Subconscious, how is the vehicle doing, how's her body, how's her emotions?

J: Her emotions always trip her up. It's the intensity of the energy being so overwhelmed in love. Being in that frequency of the fifth dimension is so good physically, it really is quite a beautiful experience to have. We have not given it to many people because those people who desperately are struggling so much...this must sound like the reverse of what we should be doing, because we know that people still have to stay here for a little bit in this density. If we keep giving them the full New Earth experience every time they are in their awakening, living their 3D best lives, it's so much harder. We're trying to prevent a lot of suicides at this moment, and we are trying to uplift the light workers who are so sick of this density. They are just wanting to end it all, and we're saying: **keep strong, keep believing in your purpose and mission here. You are so needed. You are so much more stronger than you ever believe. You are unbreakable.** You know this and you feel this, but you also feel tired, and you also feel alone, and so we say: have courage, have faith, have trust, and above all, have love. You can feel the frequency of love Source energy from here when you choose to, but so many of you won't even take the time to do a little bit of inner work, to do a little bit of praying or meditation or something to be able to stop your busy egos. Your egos are on hyperdrive, but your egos are heightened and alert because your egos are afraid of change. It's not designed to accept the shift. It's not designed to accept your physical body's leaving itself, leaving the soul. Your egos are protecting you, but it is not the protection you need. It is an old default system. It's a flawed design system now at this point. When you raise your vibrations, you can drop the ego and not pay too much attention to it. Because it's an overactive worry wart.

S: I really like the way that you mentioned it. That makes a lot of sense to me, a lot.

J: It was a great protection mechanism, and it was a way to be able to have these rudimentary lifetimes here. When you couldn't remember who your soul essence is on purpose, then you had to have another component that was taking charge. It had to be basic, it had to be rudimentary because you were only supposed to be having these rudimentary basic lives. You truly still are, you truly still are having these basic rudimentary lives, but you've made it so complicated that the ego is overworked.

S: Thank you for the information.

J: We just wanted to clarify: the ego can be overworked and humbling itself in thinking it's a terrible being and unworthy. Therefore, regardless of whether you've got a small ego or a big ego in your inflated sense of self in the 3D, you notice when there are big, true spiritual lightworkers here. They're not truly promoting themselves or their names or their brands because they are in complete balance. They don't have a big, inflated ego where they're bragging, branding, and boasting about themselves to be able to impress upon others. You know the difference between a small ego and a big ego, but we want to say: regardless of the size of your ego, they've always been overworked. It is really time to step aside, the ego to be able to go within, and truly connect into a much greater sense of self.

S: Subconscious, I have a question: if people are struggling with the ego, having such a strong position in their lives, what would be the best ways for them to push it behind them a little bit?

J: Depending on whether they've got, what you would call a small ego versus a big ego: humbling yourself if you've got the big ego to be able to realize you're just one being who is not the center of the universe, and that you all played an important piece, and you should stop trying to put other people down to make yourself feel good. The small egos, who do not think that they are even worthy to speak to someone because they can't even justify talking to someone, because they just don't feel worthy at all. It's about the accuracy of self-worth for both a small ego and a big ego, an accuracy of self-worth and self-value to humanity, as a collective to all beings here now. Do we need to explain more, or are you able to take from our recommendation?

S: Very good, yes, thank you. Very valid information. I appreciate that so much. Subconscious, I was going to ask just a curiosity question about 5D with the New Earth, when it comes to daily living? For example, I know we've explored in previous sessions, can a woman have a child on New Earth?

J: Well, first of all, you don't have daily living because there is no day. That is a reference point to a time, and it is just an awareness of the presence of being in the fifth dimension. You don't really have what you would sort of call 'night time', but you don't get tired because you're high frequency energy, so you're just living your best 5D high vibrational lives. Your day routine is not a job, it is just continually connecting with each other or connecting with your creations of flowers and plants by yourself. Not often would you want to do something by yourself because you're constantly co-creating with others, or you go and practice on your own to be able to then show others and teach others and guide others into how you created such a thing. It has to have the right integrity and the right intentions to be able to create something. A big part of your starting point on the New Earth is remembering who you are— remembering all your different lifetimes. It is important to be able to learn and grow from it, as reference points, to being able to create certain things. You could create dwellings, you could create community places, you really don't have many limitations on the way you want to exist and cohabit with others. You are not, however, cavemen-like. We understand that this has been a great concern for people to think that they are going to be having to be so basic again and learn how to survive that way. That is not the case at all. You do not need the same requirements for your bodies or your physical lives. Your life experiences in the fifth dimension are so vastly different. Your bodies are virtually self maintained through the energy frequency, but many of you still have an attachment to feeding and nurturing yourselves. There are possibilities for food nourishment. You're asking about the gender of the female energy to be able to procreate, and we say there is no longer a need for gender. You don't need to be one gender, as gender is fluid. This is why it's starting to become topical in your current day, because you have to get used to being able to be a neutral energy, whether you choose to be a masculine, feminine, or a mixture of in between. You can be that as a representation of your expression of the fifth dimension and that frequency. You are creating songs, and the songs are the expressions of the life you want to translate that frequency into. We have found ourselves in a muddle trying to express again how you live on the New Earth, because you don't need money, you don't need society structures, you don't need leaders. You are all so respected and equal and so valid to be able to grow and have shared skill sets and energy exchanges with each other. You are all trying to translate that frequency, and you're so creative with how you express yourself. It is like you all listen to one amazing song, and your bodies will respond in a certain way to express that. You will dance differently, maybe some of you are together or someone is freestyling it in a different interpretation of the song, but you're all translating this song. You're all translating that fifth dimensional energy into an expression of a way of life, one that you want, and it's surrounding you. It's how you're translating that love, that joy, their freedom and expression, and so it looks beautiful, frequency merging upon beautiful frequency, and different ways to express. When you are translating this beautiful energy into, we want to say, artworks of expression, you get to play with the energy, and define the energy, because you're light bodies, and truly the way of your life is so different. It is so hard to expand upon what a light body being really does with their time, what you would call time.

S: Thank you, it was a broad question. I was curious to know: are beings born on the New Earth, or do they will themselves to go there, and do they create themselves on the New Earth? I'm just curious about the cycle of life on it.

J: All life contracts are divinely written. All life contracts are divinely orchestrated with collectives. As a soul essence, you would still have to have a contract to go into the New Earth, and so you couldn't just choose as a free will agent of the soul essence to just pop up onto the New Earth. It is almost like 'invite only', and you must be born, and you can't be created into the New Earth as a newer energy, but it is still protected. You are asking if you could reincarnate into the New Earth, and we would say: it is somewhat similar in terms of you could energetically manifest a new being to come on to the New Earth while it is infused with a soul. Does that help?

S: Yes, sorry, it was such a broad question. It just came to my thoughts. That's very cool, though. Thank you, thank you so much.

J: It's painless to conceive and to birth. It is not the same as Earth. There is so much life. There's so many beings already on the New Earth that creating a new soul essence to come in is not very common. It is possible, but again, it's so vastly different. The New Earth, when it is seeded and populated— all those souls haven't come from Earth. There's many that actually come off other planets that will join in with soul family essences. They will merge into the New Earth, with their own crystalline bodies that haven't come from Earth, but can maintain the frequency vibration. They want to enjoy the New Earth with some soul family.

S: Wow, amazing.

J: This is why you can still see what you would perceive as 'dead people' arriving on the New Earth as orbs, because that's ultimately what your true soul essence is, it is an energy orb. You think you need to have a meat suit or a crystalline body, but when you're truly comfortable with self, you don't need to project out-loud how big your soul essence is. We say that the soul is not like the ego. You, the big egos, are trying to convince everyone, 'I'm big and important,' and the well-balanced ego is comfortable with its size. The energies of soul essences can be completely 'very high and advanced,' but it doesn't need to represent that in a size from our perspective.

S: Thank you. There is a private question from the vehicle about her parallel lifetime being on the ship. What can you tell us?

J: Yes, yes, indeed. It's a parallel lifetime, but also it's her Subconscious, her higher dimensional counterpart which you call the Arcturian. She is right, in terms of it's both soul essences coexisting together in a parallel formation, because he's living his best ninth dimensional self, and she's living the best she can in her third dimension. There are quite a few different aspects of them, which are all part of fractions of Source that have broken away. She knows this, but she wanted to figure out who it was, that being she explored in another session. She wants to know about that ship. Yes, the ship is called Athena. That is an Arcturian ship that is called Athena, but not by them. They say it was a reference to remind her. She always knew that there was something significant about the name Athena. There is nothing of urgency that she needs. We want to remind her about how it was that they did uplift people from Atlantis, which was energetically removing their souls, but they also removed their physical bodies as well onto the ship. This is how some people will take their full bodies with them. We take their full bodies onto the ships, and the 3D, their physical carbon-based bodies, to some degree, some of the density has been pulled off then. They do not breathe anymore, but they are less carbon-based than they were on Earth. While on the ship, they are still transitioning, and they still have implants of, what you would call, your 'chakra systems' that are crystals. They are in your body in their actual energetic crystals, which are your chakra systems, that then get removed from the overlay of the physical body that you're projecting as a physical body. When those chakra systems are taken off you, which is our design for the bodies as part of the experience, these are how you have the veil of forgetfulness. They block your memory. Once removed, the soul gains memory of who you are, and then the soul is able to remember what their purpose and other lives have been and currently are. It's all designed to be fun, they said with laughter, but it got a bit out of hand. You have that full transfusion on the ships. The med beds are also part of that, to heal the soul, to remove all the density fragments, the half 'yuck' density that didn't break away from the full physical body. The med beds then acclimates and re-calibrates your crystalline body back into function, then transmutes it into another natural form. When you are in a ninth dimension, you are still not just the consciousness. You are still a being, but you are working on even getting comfortable with your own representations. We are who we are. Our energy is comfortable to what we want to appear to each other as. The fifth dimension is different, because you're just merging with energy, and you're just trying to settle into not being as physical as you think. You are sort of learning about the bigger energy field. It is so overwhelming that you're all merging with energies as one. You actually want to evolve to be able to harness all of that energy, but be more a singular physical reality, while you are so much more in the 5D than in the 3D. Because it is not controlled as much. It's not explored as much. It's not mastered on an independent level. So you explore and learn these skill sets, but you don't want to keep being merged together in this training dimension as a whole, when you gain your own life contract lessons. It is really paradise, in terms of a holiday. This is why we gave the reference of being champagne on the most beautiful beach in the world, because it's luxury to be able to not have any worries in the fifth dimension. Really, it is paradise. You just try to master the energy to remember who you are, to remember how powerful you are, to remember how you can create and manipulate energy. When you go back into those higher dimensions, you are skilled to manage what is next. When you go up into those higher dimensions, you are truly more of a service and help assisting other planets. To be able to evacuate them when needed. To be able to be guides for others. To be able to maintain many other beings' experiences on many other planets. We feel like we overspoke, and you did not ask us such questions.

S: It's all amazing. Thank you.

J: We're showing it to the vehicle. While it makes complete utter sense to her now, but we know when she listens back, it's going to be very surreal.

S: Indeed, definitely something to process.

J: The beauty of these senses and this information is: she will always remember what we're showing her. Then she may doubt it or fuddle or get confused along the way, but this has been recorded for her to remember the power of the excitements that lay ahead.

S: Wonderful, yes, thank you. Thank you so much.

Session 3

J: I'd like to call upon the Subconscious, please?

C: Yes, we're here.

J: Wonderful, thank you so much. Are you able to do a body scan for the vehicle, and tell me what is happening to her body?

C: She is very relaxed, always, well there are a few pains and niggles. They are the connections that she has with what's going on around her and around the world at the moment. She's quite busy at the moment.

J: What is she doing at the moment to be so busy?

C: She is sharing her light. She is releasing the dense energy on this planet. She is supporting people, many, many people. She is supporting this planet. She is supporting a lot. And when she comes back, when she is here in her 3D life, she still has a lot of chords and connections with what she is doing. And that gives her pain. But we tell her that she can ask for this to be eased. But sometimes, when she just knows that she's being of support and service to a lot of situations on this planet, that just gives her inner peace, and she doesn't worry about it. But there isn't a lot of work she is doing at the moment with this planet. And there are beings on this planet that she is supporting, and not all of them are spiritual people or know anything about it, so that is what they're supposed to be. It's their contract to be like that. She is part of her family. There's a lot.

J: Okay, well, are you able to help support and heal and balance her body completely, and remove everything that no longer serves her physically, as we continue on with this session today?

C: Yes.

J: Thank you so much. Subconscious, am I able to ask what dimension you are in?

C: We are in the 12th dimension.

J: Thank you so much. From your perspective Subconscious, in terms of the "shift" what does that mean? Shifting to the fifth dimension for humanity.

C: There is so much that we see that can be gained for humanity from shifting into the fifth dimension. There is inner peace, there is love, there's companionship. There's awareness and a connection back to who they are. It has been a great purpose of lessons learned being here on 3D planet Earth. But it hasn't evolved as it should have. The lessons have been hard and traumatic. Being in the fifth dimension, the lessons that will be learned will be different, but very purposeful. It will be less traumatic. There will be no traumatic events. And all the lessons that they've learned here will be in their records — so that they will never forget the trauma, the hardship, and the heartache. And they will be able to help others and other planets and other beings. It's very important that humanity and beings that are on this planet at the moment, going through the hardship that they're going through, is so very, very, very important, but it will help many galaxies and many beings. It is purposeful, but very hard. And they will become very sought after beings with the experiences that they have had. Many galaxies are watching over planet Earth at the moment. Many galaxies are seeing what people, humanity and beings are going through. And sometimes it makes their hearts ache, because they know they could never do this. So all that is here at the moment is being held in very high regards, and the lessons and experiences that are going to be able to be shared and acknowledged and accessed for many, many, many lifetimes to come. The people in the future will be in awe that other beings went through what they're going through now. It is not something that we wanted, but it is something that has happened. These records will be always there for many, many, many beings and many lifetimes to come. With lessons learned, experiences had, and achievements overcome. And a shift with 3D and their love and then to shift to 5D and be love. It is a great, great, great achievement.

J: Thank you, and so how will people notice that they have shifted into the fifth dimension?

C: They will see with their eyes, they will feel with their bodies. It is not something that they won't know. It will be like night and day. They will realize on this Earth it was like night. It's dark and dense. Sometimes you have to feel what you're doing because you can't see. And sometimes you're feeling lost when you're here on this planet, and you don't really fully understand. And sometimes you're just walking around in the dark blindly. When they are on the ships, the light will come into their beingness. And then when they are presented to the New Earth, the vibration, the frequency, the love, the light, the brightness, it is not something that you can miss. It is so beautiful and so profound. It will be filled with joy. It will be filled with love and anticipation and excitement, like all their dreams coming true. They will start to remember who they were and their purpose and they will be proud of themselves. They will honor themselves, and they will think how great they were to achieve what they have achieved here. There will be many meetings and many conversations on the New Earth and to talk about them, experiences and their lives, but there will be no dense energy. Plans being made and conversations of their lives will be talked about. This New Earth is not going to be like shifting from one city to another. There's new things to be built, sorted, organized. It's like going on a camping trip. You have all that you need around you, you just have to put it all together and build it, and be with one with it all. It is not something that you can miss. You will be in total awe of what you feel and see. And even in the transition time of leaving this planet to traveling, there will be moments of doubt, there will be moments of fear and anxiety. But these will be very quickly and easily understood and overcome. There will be joy, there will be happiness, there will be inner peace, there will be remembrance. Reconnections with loved ones from other lifetimes, in your soul families, that will be beautiful, the reconnection. And then when you start to remember, you will be grateful.

J: Thank you so much. Can you tell me please, Subconscious, about the life contract for this planet, the soul of this planet, in terms of shifting to the fifth dimension? What can you tell us about the soul of the planet's contract?

C: It was not fulfilled, the dense energy got too much for her. It was hard, but like many beings on this planet, you adjust to the hardness and the dense energy, and it becomes the new normal. And then you just do the best you can with what you've got around you. This is what happened to Gaia. Her new normal was not what she wanted in her contract. But she accepts that they were all lessons that were learned, so many lessons learned. She is in a better place now. She's merging with a new planet, the New Earth, she's reconnecting in there. She's becoming one with it. She has a golden thread connecting to this planet. A part of her is still here and that part is being protected. She is one of those beings with others who are protecting this part, and the golden thread that is through a portal. It is very, very encased and protected. Gaia is going well, she is rejoicing and enjoying the New Earth which she is part of now. She's not fully part of it, but she has moved up to the fifth dimension in it, and she is a higher, stronger being for it. And she has more skills that she can take care of this planet, the Old Earth that is now. She's been upgraded so that she can do both. It's no bother for her, it's quite easy as she moves through and enjoys the fifth dimension frequencies on this new planet. She is healed and healing well. She comes in to many people and talks to them and tells them she is well. She is happy. She is in a good place. She's preparing the New Earth for the arrival of the beings, and there are others there with her who are helping. There are many higher dimensional beings there, too, surrounding the planet helping. It is becoming very close to being ready to receive, the waters are flowing and crystal-clear trees are bright. The atmosphere and the frequency, it's quite beautiful. There are flowers in the meadows and in the fields. Gaia is nearly ready and she is aware of what she went through. And she has the utmost respect, acknowledgement, compassion, forgiveness and understanding for all what happened, that all is in a better place now. There is so much happening. So many portals open, so many golden threads from this planet to the New Earth. There are so many beings protecting these portals. There is so much protection and high energies on this planet that is needed to be—so it doesn't fall apart. The natural disasters are being held down. She is helping them hold them down. It is not time for the majority to shift yet, but it is very soon. There is so much going on, so, so much going on.

J: Thank you so much. Subconscious, what is the term Old Earth referring to?

C: Old Earth means that there is no soul in the planet, there is no light in the planet core, the being has completely gone.

J: Thank you, so there is still a future event that humanity will experience living on this planet without the soul of the planet being connected?

C: Gaia has evolved so much that she herself was not expected to have the abilities that she has now, and the portals to be connected to this planet and just the tiniest spark is all this planet needs. But even when the natural disasters and the laser happened, it was going to be to release her, so that she may totally shift to the New Earth. But things have changed. She has abilities that are just more than what was expected. So the laser and that will release the dense energies out of the planet, and it no longer needs to release Gaia. Because it's only a little spark. But she would take more with her when the laser does happen. It will be just the tiniest little flicker, like the candle is going out, but it's just got a little bit more light there. She will hold that there because it's not a burden on her. She can help those ones on the Old Earth with just this tiny little bit of light. And when everyone, near everyone shifts, she will call that back. And that's when this planet will get quite dark and very empty, and there will be very few people left on this planet that will experience that. But she is able to help support just the tiniest bit, the people on the Old Earth having the Old Earth experience. But it won't be for long. She loves them so much that she is able to support them with just the tiniest bit of energy. And then they will come to her, too. And there will be joy and happiness. She is very different. She is very, very different now. She can do a lot more than what she could before.

J: Could you give me examples of how she's different now?

C: She doesn't have any dense energies or lower vibrations. Her frequency is high. She is happy that the skills here, the connections that she has to the Earth, the New Earth, are such high frequency connections. It is very hard to explain; it's just energy. When Gaia was to arrive at New Earth, she was to connect in with it and become one with the planet. And she has done this, and then it has evolved and evolved more and more than what was expected. And as she has evolved and become one with the planet, and the trees, and the water, the animals, and the birds, it has become to such a high beautiful frequency that it is more, more than what was ever thought possible. So that it is even more, it is even more and better and beautiful and she has new abilities and skills that she is honing in on or perfecting. That she could have never, ever thought possible here on this planet. The New Earth is even more than what was ever thought possible. It's even more than what a lot of us thought possible. It is frequency, it is energy, it is light. It is truly, truly magnificent. That's why Gaia has been able to connect and stay with the Old Earth easily. It's not a burden. We never realized the magnificence or the possibilities of this transition and change, and what could become. It is a new lesson that we are all witnessing. New possibilities, when all this energy, high frequencies, there is fifth dimension, and then there is fifth dimension on the New Earth. It is truly, truly magnificent. More, more than what we expected, more than what we anticipated. The possibilities are just magnificent. That's why people will notice. That's why beings will notice. That's why in the portals at the moment, there are beings who are on this planet that have the threads connected to the New Earth. And that energy is coming back from the New Earth to this planet and supporting it. But not just the planet, the beings on here and humanity. Because if it wasn't so, dense energies and destructions would have been quite a lot. We see no purpose in the beings on this planet now that are going through what they're going through now to be traumatized by destruction. It is all different. There are lessons that they're going through. There is intense change happening, intense change happening on this planet. And it's been able to be done very successfully and easily. With the threads that are connected to the New Earth and this planet here and the beings that are being supported and the light frequencies that are coming onto this planet, are high intense energies—so much that we could never have thought possible. It is all so, so beautiful. It's also magnificent. But some of the beings on this planet have other beings who are part of that 3D on this planet, part of them have moved in, to help hold this frequency from the New Earth, and share it around, because they're physical 3D bodies could not hold this frequency. They might be in 3D bodies, but their connection to their teams, their highest self and to the New Earth, is so high that these other beings have to be part of that 3D person. Otherwise they'd be just like a balloon, they would just pop, and therefore the connection would be severed. This is part of these magnificent possibilities that we can do now. It is magnificent. It is profound. It is beautiful. It is more than what we ever thought possible, and there is so much light. So much light is being shared around. It is a lot. It is not really explainable. Is not what we even thought possible last year. The possibilities, the progress, has changed so much.

J: It is fantastic to hear, thank you so much. From your perspective, Subconscious, what are some of the lessons for people experiencing the Old Earth?

C: Always different for a lot of people. They need to let go of physical things. They need to let go of things that they've held so dear that are physical. They need to reconnect with themselves, and they need to reconnect with others. They need to become one with others. Need to trust and love themselves. They need to become a community, and not be living in isolation with all their worldly physical possessions. And not thinking money, a big house, fast flash cars are important. They need to learn that these are not important. People, communities, and themselves are important. To stop punishing themselves for not achieving the great things that they wanted to achieve, which is just physical. They will learn to love themselves. They will learn to trust their intuition. They will learn to be one and share with others and be part of a community group where there is friendship, sharing, trust, companionship, and a belief that there are great things for them. And that they have a connection to Source. They have an understanding that their lives on this planet were just for a short time, that they are part of something a lot bigger than what they ever could imagine. They will accept and understand this. They will know, they will feel the support of their teams, and they will know and understand and be grateful. Things are going to be very different to what the Old Earth experiences were going to be, as far as how people will be coping and feeling and understanding. It is not filled with fear, filled with anger, filled with hate. This is a dense energy, and when the laser happens, this dense energy will be transmuted to Source. The experiences will be different than what was first thought. There will still be time for adjustments.

J: Thank you. Subconscious, how would you like her and her family to prepare for their Old Earth experience?

C: We are in constant communication with her, and she is preparing things. She can buy food, cans of food. Messages we tell her, messages she receives. It is enough, she doesn't need to prepare a lot. She will be supporting a lot of people. She will have a lot of food. She can support people and feed them. In her area, they have several factories. There will not be a great deal of food or water shortages. There will be destruction around them. People will come together and support. People will support one another and those who are afraid, they will see the groups gathered, and they will come into those groups because they will feel the energy. They will hear the laughter and the talking in the chatter and want to be part of that group. There will be lots of groups around. And she is to play a big part in those groups. She will be doing lots of walking. She will be going around and talking to many people. She will be sharing their knowledge, she'll be sharing the light and the love. She will be very busy. She is also one who has a connection to the new planet, and she will be bringing in the energies to those groups. They will feel the energy on the New Earth, and they will know that it's okay and they are okay. And they will be preparing themselves to change their thoughts, mindsets, their actions, because they will feel some of what these frequencies and energies on the New Earth are like. And each group, as they get to a certain frequency—they won't be left here, they will be lifted off. And it won't be in a natural disaster, they will just be lifted, they will go on to their ships. This will be a smooth transition. We see her traveling far, not just in her community. We see her traveling long distances and being very busy. She needs to share the energy, the frequencies from New Earth with many groups, many areas, and many places. This will lift their vibration and their frequencies. And they will shift off effortlessly. This is the way it's going to be now, sometimes she will drive, sometimes she will walk.

J: Thank you, she was curious about power. Would she need alternative methods of power? What can you tell her about her Old Earth experience?

C: There will be power around her, there will be restrictions on the amount of power, but they will have power for certain times of the day. There are other methods that she can use to keep her freezes going which have got food in them. And help support some of the petrol pumps, so they can pump fuel out, but it will be restricted. But also there will be very little traffic. Because a lot of people's cars now are all computerized and connected to computers. There will be internet, there will be some phone services, but the technology to run these cars will not be working. It is not necessary for people's computerized cars to be working. There are enough older vehicles around, and they will be able to use the fuel, and they will get around. The others will walk, the others will just stay put. Those that need to travel around, will have the vehicles to travel around in. Because they're not computerized, they are very, very old vehicles, and they will be able to be used.

J: Can you give me an understanding of what event took place for the modern vehicles that use computers to no longer be working?

C: The lasers. They will take out a lot of towers and infrastructure that run these vehicles. They are not needed. They are held too high in people's priorities of being important in their lives. They need to know that they are not. So when they are not able to be used, they will know that they are not as important in their lives as what they first thought. And they need to change their priorities to something else. They need to walk.

J: Fantastic, okay, thank you so much. Such interesting information. Can you, Subconscious, please define and explain to me more about the New Earth? You said it was a separate Earth from this planet. Why is there the need for this new planet, this New Earth?

C: The planets in this galaxy are too dense. There used to be life on many other planets in this galaxy. But actions by some mean life is no longer. Planet Earth is the last one to have life in it. So New Earth could not be in this galaxy, as it is too dense. It had to be in a different galaxy, and there are different planets in this distant, different galaxy. They are all new, they are all being created. It is important that the dense energy in this galaxy stays here. It has to be, to be able to move forward with love and light. And to make progressions in many new ways of doing things. The dense energy has to stay in this galaxy. So a New Earth, the new galaxy was planned, and now it is actualized. It is immensely more than we ever anticipated that it could possibly be. This new galaxy, with this New Earth, with this magnificence of what is happening now. There are other planets in that galaxy being developed. They are currently also being built and made. The work and what has happened to the New Earth and how it has developed, has been so immensely successful. The progressive Gaia is making it, we have decided, many have decided, that the New Earth is not going to be the only new planet in that galaxy. There are certainly going to be many others. There will be a 3D planet in this new galaxy that will not have any dense energies. It will be a place for 3D beings to be and live out their lives. There will be other planets, and we're still sorting this out at the moment. But the prospects of what could be, without this dense energy, is just so magnificent that we are not just stopping with the New Earth, and we are not just stopping with one planet in this new galaxy. It is progressing so well that we are so pleased. We are so very, very pleased that there will be many other planets in this new galaxy. But the dense energies have to stay in this galaxy. It cannot escape, it will be entrapped. We know now how to do this, and we can do it. It will be entrapped in this galaxy, and this galaxy will get smaller and smaller, and the dense energies will no longer exist. There are many beings who are working with us now, and we have all just started on this dense energy. It serves no planet. It serves no purpose for any galaxies. It will be transformed, it will be transformed, into light and love. We can do this now. We have the abilities, and this galaxy will no longer exist. But it will not blow up, it will be transformed. It is quite amazing. We are very pleased. We feel that this is such a good thing. But that is why the planet, the New Earth, could not be in this galaxy—because it would eventually go down the same path. The dense energies have no purpose on the New Earth or the new galaxies. There are some other galaxies that do have dense energies but not as bad as this. We know now dense energy cannot continue. It can be changed. It will be changed.

J: Thank you so much, that is such wonderful news. I really appreciate that. Subconscious, can you explain to me the main differences between the carbon-based bodies that we're in now and the crystalline-based bodies that we are hearing about?

C: [Laughter] What is the difference between the dark and what is the difference between the light?! When you get up in the morning you see the sun, the sun is warm, it is shining bright. There is lightness, there's brightness, it's different. When you're in the dark, it is night. When the moon is not shining and there's clouds to hide the stars, it is darkness. You have your senses, you know who you are, you know you are your body—but you don't know where you're going or what you're doing. You have to navigate with great difficulty. Everything is uncertain, you do not see. You walk around and you bump into something it hurts. There is a difference between night and day. There is such a profound difference between a 3D dense body and a light body. Some people will take their bodies, because they need to have them. And they will understand and make the transition slower. But then their 3D bodies will slowly change. The 3D bodies that are on this planet now, the ones you call the meat suits, are very, very important. They're not worthless, they're not rubbish. They will not be chucked onto the heaps. The DNA and the energy and the information that are in them, will be kept. We will store them. And if people want their bodies, they can. They will not go to 5D Earth with these bodies. But some people, when they shift, they will realize, it's like wearing a big heavy coat. And they will think after a while, 'this is a heavy coat, I want to take it off,' and they will take it off. And they will understand that what they were carrying was a 3D body, and it no longer serves them. And they will be in their form of light bodies, which will be different for many, depending where they're going and what they're doing. Some light bodies are very light, some light bodies are very crystalline light. But there is too much, too much difference. This body is like a heavy coat. You are carrying it because it serves a purpose. When that time comes, you will be happy to take it off. There will be no fear, all is well.

J: Wonderful, thank you so much. We hear many other people talking about the New Earth being here now on this planet and that we...

C: [Laughter] we hear them talking too! The time is coming.

J: So we hear that they're telling us that we are now in the 5D. Where are they getting their information from?

C: Sometimes it is important for them to feel this, because without it, they will not raise their vibration and their frequency. The people that they are telling this to are the people that need to hear this. It is helping raise their frequency. It is important for them to do this, to raise their frequency. And when they have risen to a certain frequency, because they've been following these people who are telling them that they are shifted onto 5D on this planet, when they have raised their frequency enough, they will realize that these people that are talking to them and telling them that 5D is here, they'll realize that it's not true. But when you are in a dense, lost, low place and if the thought that you can move into a higher 5D frequency is a possibility of your thoughts and your feelings and how you treat yourself and how you treat others, it's a possibility of moving into—then this is important. It's important to raise their frequency. Some people, some beings who are speaking these words, they must continue to do this. It is important that they do this because those who are traveling on their stepping stones, they need to go through the possibilities of believing that they can and they are able to reach 5D. And when they do and feel that they are in that place, sometimes it's better that they just stay in that frequency, because it helps, keeps them in that high vibration frequency, and their minds are positive. There are others who are preaching it. When the time is right, they will be exposed. But people need these stepping stones to travel on, to get to the ability and the knowingness and the understanding that they can, and it is possible.

J: Thank you so much. Is there any other information you would like to share with us today?

C: Many things have changed. So much that it is not possible to discuss it all. It serves no purpose to discuss it all. What was said, what was thought, 12 months or your two years ago, is very different now. Lessons are learnt through understanding, compassion, and love, and can be done quite differently and easily. There is a purpose for a lot of things happening and those purposes are important. If it is not in dense energy, and it is not dense, it is not of fear, and it is not promoting fear, then it has a purpose. It is important. Because for some people, it is not possible to hear and understand all the information that is being shared of moving to another planet and going into 5D on another planet. They cannot comprehend, they cannot cope, they would go into fear. But if somebody says to them, 'you could go into 5D, raise your mindset, raise your thoughts, have high frequency thoughts and feelings'—and then they do. And they feel good! And then they start telling everybody, 'you just need to do this, you just need to do that' and others will go, 'Well that's a lot of hogwash. What about all the horrible things that are happening on this planet? How can that possibly be that this planet is in 5D?' And they have that mindset because that's what they need to do. They have been guided to the areas and the people that are sharing the correct information. But for that person who is in that mindset of being in 5D, they are being of support, they are being of love, they are being of compassion and they are supporting. They might not be speaking the truth of what you know, but they are speaking the truth of what they know. And they are speaking the truth of what others need to hear. That is all purposeful, it is all supportive. When it is time, these others will hear what they need to hear. But if you are not preaching fear, if you are not projecting doubt, if you are not preaching disasters and horrible things happening to everybody—but you are telling them to raise your frequency, you can move into 5D—this is important for them. It is raising frequencies. When the time is right, they will be ready to know the next step, and they will move into the next step. There is a lot of dense energy, but it's not controlling people. People are controlling people. People are controlling their own minds and their own thoughts, and they are being guided in the direction that serves them. And what serves one will not necessarily serve the other.

J: Thank you so much. Really appreciate all the information you've given to us today. So we will ask you to recede to where you belong with much love and appreciation for the information you have shared with us. I know when we listen back to this material and put it into place, we'll really appreciate and be able to apply all the information you've provided for us.

Session 4

J: Subconscious, can you tell me what is happening to the body please?

L: Her hands have been sore.

J: What's happening there for her?

L: She loves giving massages to help a lot of people at work and she doesn't do it properly. She knows this. Her hands are sore from that.

J: I see, so it's purposeful that you remind her of that. Are you able to help release that now that she's learned this lesson?

L: Yes.

J: Thank you. What else is happening for her body?

L: She is very calm and relaxed.

J: Beautiful. Is there anything else you can help heal or balance or release in her body?

L: She's been releasing density from her digestive system.

J: Is there anything you'd like her to know about that?

L: Drink more water.

J: Subconscious, how much water would you like her to drink?

L: She drinks a lot of water. She needs to infuse her water with more energy and love and intention. She drinks enough water, she just needs to focus on infusing it with love and healing energy for herself.

J: Wonderful. Thank you very much, and may she be reminded of this regularly when she goes to grab water—that it needs to be infused with love.

L: Yes, yes.

J: Beautiful, thank you so much, Subconscious. Is there anything else you're going to do to help heal and balance your body today?

L: She needs to focus on cleansing between her clients again. She gets lazy with it, and then she doesn't feel so good the next day.

J: How is the best way for her to cleanse between clients?

L: She's been doing it, and it's effective when she does it. She imagines water falling over her body and helps us to remove any density. Sometimes she gets lazy, and she'll look at her phone for a few minutes instead of clearing the density. So, I need to remind her to keep on clearing that density. It helps her with her headaches on the days after she works.

J: I see. Is there anything else you would like her to know about her body, Subconscious?

L: It is working well.

J: Wonderful. Subconscious, I'd like to know what dimension you are in?

L: Seven popped up. (7th dimension)

J: Thank you so much. Subconscious, from your perspective, in terms of the "shift", what does shifting to 5D mean for humanity?

L: It means evolution, a natural process where humanity is intended to go. You're not intended to just stay stagnant. We need to grow. Everybody needs to grow, no matter where you are. You need to grow and move on, and the next evolutionary step is moving from this 3D to the next 5D.

J: I see. Thank you so much. Is there anything else you'd like to share with us about the shift for humanity?

L: It's going to be beautiful. Everybody's going to go where they belong. Not all will shift to 5D, and that's okay.

J: Could you say that they potentially shift to other 3D planets or beyond 5D according to their life contracts?

L: Yes. Some will go back to where they came from, which may be 7D or back to Source. Some will continue learning lessons in 3D, and some will go to 5D to experience that, just to see what it is like. Those may stay longer, or they may go after being there for a short time.

J: Thank you so much. Subconscious, in terms of the life contract for this planet's soul, in terms of shifting to the 5D, what would you like me to know about the life contract for what we call Gaia moving to the fifth dimension?

L: Her contract has changed a lot over the last many years. Humanity is so embedded with her consciousness, and has had such a big impact on her and her body that she wasn't able to do what she really wanted to do here. So, we gave her other options, and she decided she wanted to move to a different 5D planet.

J: Thank you.

L: She is very excited.

J: Tell me more about that.

L: She is looking forward to having us all on her new, beautiful body. She is excited to try to provide for us as a whole and for us to learn higher vibrational lessons—joy and love.

J: Thank you. Subconscious, what does the term Old Earth refer to?

L: She (the vehicle) thinks of it as after a laser event, but we've already started having tastes of Old Earth now. Instead of a few individuals experiencing much longer time on Old Earth, many more people are experiencing tastes of what Old Earth is like. Changes like lack of food and lack of resources, this is the start of Old Earth. It officially starts when Gaia's soul totally leaves at the laser event, but much of what is happening now was intended to happen on Old Earth.

J: Thank you. Can you please give me some examples of the life lessons people want to experience on the Old Earth?

L: Connections and helping each other. Everyone is going to be distraught in some way, and people are going to come together and love and support each other. People will learn not to fear each other any longer. Humanity has been learning to fear and distrust each other because of this virus that has gotten so much attention. People need to connect again. Many people are very disconnected from their teams as well, and they will ask us for help then.

J: Thank you so much. Is there anything else you'd like us to know about the experience on Old Earth?

L: It's going to be challenging. But, when the beings who are experiencing Old Earth are done with it, they are going to be so proud of themselves that they did what they did. Once they get through that, they can get through anything.

J: Thank you so much. Subconscious, in terms of the New Earth, what is New Earth?

L: It's very green and pristine and beautiful. The water is blue. Pollution will not be allowed. It is a beautiful place. It is the body of Gaia, a new body. It's reincarnation into the next level for her, and the next level for us as well.

J: Thank you so much. In terms of the different ways that we would be living on the New Earth compared to the Old Earth, what are some of the things you'd like us to know?

L: It's going to be like night and day. It's going to be so different. Humanity doesn't know what it's like NOT to be controlled. On New Earth they will have free will and they will not be controlled. That will not be allowed. They will have free will, but there are things that will not be allowed to happen.

J: Thank you, wonderful. Can you please give the vehicle a peek at the New Earth and can you tell me what she senses and notices when she arrives there?

L: It's absolutely beautiful. She's in a meadow and there are trees in the distance. The sky looks like crystal. It's the perfect temperature, it's just a nice breeze. Everything's so vibrant. The colors are beautiful. There are colors there that humans have never seen. It is such a beautiful place. We're all excited to move everyone there.

J: How does she feel sensing into that energy of the fifth dimension?

L: Her whole body's tingly. She's very excited! She knows there's work to do here, but she's very excited about the New Earth.

J: Fantastic! Subconscious, can you tell me about the bodies that we will be in or feel attached to on the New Earth?

L: They're called crystalline for a reason. They're crystal based, they're not carbon based.

J: What would they look like from our perspective? Would they look like our forms in the carbon base that we portray ourselves to be in our current vehicles?

L: We can if we want. We can change what we look like, because appearance isn't important there. We can look how we choose to look. When people first get there, they will look like they do in 3D. Once they get comfortable with everything, they can learn how to transform their appearance in any way they want. It's more energetic. It's an energetic place, so light.

J: Wonderful. Can the bodies that we're in now, the carbon-based bodies, go to New Earth?

L: No, the carbon based bodies are 3D bodies. It doesn't make sense for them to be on a 5D planet. It's not possible. You can have a crystalline body that appears to look similar to your 3D body, which most people will have when they first get there, but you can't have your physical body that you have right now on New Earth.

J: So it will appear as if it is the carbon-based body, when it really is truly the illusion that the crystalline body is presenting to each other?

L: No, it'll look different. If she (the vehicle) chooses to look the same as her current appearance, she can have the same features, shape and hair, but it will look different.

J: Thank you so much, Subconscious. Many people who are talking about the New Earth are stating that it is here, now, on this planet that we're living on and that we are currently in the fifth dimension. Where are they getting their information?

L: They are getting it from different "sources." For one, it depends on their collective. It could also be due to their ego. Some collectives are not moving on to 5D, so their next progression is a 3D planet, and that seems like very "out there" information, so they say it's here. In regards to the ego—many people have attachments here. They've made a lot of wealth here. They're scared to go. Fear is holding them back. There are different factors or reasons that people are saying that 5D is here, now, but it's clearly not here. There is no famine, no money, no extinction, no control or rulers in 5D. You can have a 5D mindset here, which is very beneficial, but we're not living in the 5th dimension here.

J: Thank you. Subconscious, is there any other information you'd like us to know about this shift or New Earth or Old Earth or our physical bodies?

L: It will do nothing to fear when it starts happening. It's going to be like ripping off a band-aid. It'll be intense for a moment, but it'll be fine. It'll be wonderful afterwards. Everybody's taken care of, everybody has a place to go. Everybody is cared for and everybody has a team. There's no need to fear it and there's no need to be impatient. It'll happen when it happens. It'll be perfect timing for everybody.

J: Thank you so much. I really appreciate all the information and confirmation that you've given us today.

Session 5

J: I'd like to call upon the Subconscious, please.

S: Yes.

J: Thank you. Are you able to do a body scan on the vehicle, and tell me what is happening for her?

S: She is very tired, and she is experiencing a lot of head pressure. And a lot of throat pressure. And her chest is very tight.

J: Okay, can you tell me what's the significance of all of that, please?

S: We are purging her.

J: Can you help me understand that more?

S: She has many toxins in her body, and we are trying to purge as fast as possible.

J: What is the significance of trying to do that as fast as possible?

S: She has much work to do, and this is hindering her work.

J: What sort of work is she doing?

S: She is a lightworker, and she is not shining as bright as she normally does. And we are trying to detox the heavy metals that are currently inside of her.

J: Okay, where did she get those heavy metals from?

S: From consumption, from food, and from drinks.

J: Mmm, hmm. How are you able to detox her from those heavy metals?

S: She is finding that it is being released from all points of her body, but at a rapid rate.

J: Okay, what would you advise her to do to be able to help assist with this process?

S: She needs to drink more water—as much as she possibly can.

J: What is your advisable amount of water for her to consume per day?

S: She needs to drink between two and three liters.

J: Is this throughout the day or a special time of day?

S: She needs to drink it throughout the day and not in one go.

J: Fantastic, thank you so much. What about the headache? What's going on there?

S: She is getting lots of downloads, and it's coming in at an overwhelming pace, which is pushing the toxins out. She sees light around her, flashes of light, so she knows that she is getting her downloads. And it's an excessive amount all in one go. There is an urgency to download her very quickly.

J: Why is it an emergency situation? What's the rush?

S: She needs to have as much and as quickly as possible before she shifts.

J: Why the sudden rush?

S: You see, the things that she is being downloaded can only be accessed in the 3D world for her.

J: Okay, thank you, and what about the pain in the chest near her heart or her heart pain today? She said she's never experienced anything like that before. What's going on there?

S: We have heard her feel that she felt alone, and we are prodding her to tell her that we are here, and we are there in her heart. We are all there with her, and she is never alone.

J: I think you're prompting her with your love—actually, physically pained her, though, and this can be very confusing for the 3D vehicle.

S: Yes, but she paid attention, which is something she doesn't always do. [Laughter]

J: I see, okay, so would it be advisable for the vehicle to trust that she is always loved and never alone—for her to not experience that discomfort again when you give her a little shake up?

S: Yes, that would be more preferable, yes.

J: Fantastic, is there anything else that's going on for her body, Subconscious, that you'd like me to know?

S: She is emanating an energy source, and there are particles coming from her that are being sent into the ethers. And these particles are meeting up with other people's particles, and they are shining their lights together to an even brighter light.

J: Fantastic, are you able to balance and harmonize and strengthen and heal all of her physical body in the best way that you can, please, Subconscious?

S: Yes, we can do that.

J: Thank you, is there anything else you'd like me to know about her body?

S: She is being prepared, and she needs to know that she just needs to trust and have no fear.

J: Wonderful. Feels like she's always doing so well with that—the best we can in the 3D.

S: Yes, she's doing very well.

J: Wonderful, thank you, Subconscious. Can you tell me, please, what dimension are you in?

S: Fifth.

J: Wonderful, thank you very much. Subconscious, from your perspective, in terms of the shift, what does the shift mean? What does shifting to 5D mean for humanity?

S: Shift means a higher state of consciousness where we will be removed from Earth to New Earth. This is an experience that we have all been waiting for, and we have chosen to experience. We will be taken out of the fear and the density and into the light that is a part of our birthright—into the light, back to our homes to where we belong. This is coming very soon.

J: Thank you, and is there anything else you'd like us to know about this shift?

S: Our frequencies are being aligned—the frequency codes that we have been given when we came down to this 3D planet are being awakened. They are ready to be matched up to the ships when they come to collect. There are people that will go on to the ships with their light bodies, and there are people that will go straight to source or to where they came from, and where they call home. **We wish humanity to hold the faith and hope, and to try and remember where they came from—and to not let that light go out, but to shine that light as brightly as they can—and to have the hope and faith their light codes and their frequencies will shine brighter so that it matches up to the frequency when we come to pick them up and take them to a place that they can never imagine in their wildest dreams how magical it is.** Although we know the magic is inside them, but they will physically see the magic when they arrive to their destination.

J: Thank you so much, and in terms of Gaia, this planet's soul, what can you tell us about her life contract to shift to the fifth dimension?

S: She did not realize that it would be so dense here on Earth. She was hoping that it would go on forever and ever, because it just got far too much for her, and she was so bitterly disappointed and upset that humanity did it to themselves. And there was no saving, no saving the 3D. She chose to change her contracts and leave, but she is watching what is happening, as are we all. We're all there watching what is happening and sending as much love to every single soul that is here experiencing it. That is part of their life contracts. Gaia is safe, watching from afar, but still very connected as her heart is connected, because she's been here for so long. She is very proud of the people that have held the light, and wishes with all our heart that the people that have closed off their hearts will open them up again and just be and feel how amazing they are inside, and to not fight it, to go with the flow, and to find their inner love and their inner wisdom and to not lose faith, because there is something magical out there. She knows what is awaiting humanity on the other side.

J: Beautiful, thank you so much, is there anything else you'd like us to know about that?

S: She has felt the pain of mankind. She has felt the denseness of mankind, and she knows what you are all going through. She has so much empathy, but she has true belief that we will find inner truth and that inner love. The process you're going through is all meaningful and purposeful, and to not give up. Do not give up, because it is coming sooner than you think, and it is going to be absolutely amazing.

J: Thank you so much. Subconscious, in terms of the term Old Earth, what is that referring to?

S: Old Earth is the Earth that is left behind when the people have left and shifted. The Old Earth is the process where the trees have been taken to the New Earth, and the Old Earth is the dissolvement of things, things that are going to be dissolved into Old Earth before it leaves that orbit, where it is a closing down of the atmosphere, the closing down of everything. It will slowly dissolve into itself before it is taken away to be renovated in another solar system.

J: Okay, thank you so much. In terms of the Old Earth experience, will people be having that Old Earth experience?

S: Some will choose to stay and be there to experience everything shutting down, and some will choose to go in different directions, but they have been those souls that are dedicated to stay here on the 3D to help it dissolve—to be there in the last moments as some souls have done with many other planets—been there at the very last minute when the planet has been dissolved before in many lifetimes.

J: Thank you. Can you give me some examples of what people would want to learn and experience on the Old Earth, please?

S: They want to experience what humanity has done—the pain that they have bought amongst everything, the egos, the people that don't have compassion—that they can see what they have done, that they have destroyed, they have taken over. Their egos have so taken over that they have been blinded to what they really have come here to do— to be connected with humanity. They need to feel that denseness. They can't feel that dense when they're in ego, because their ego is hiding their innermost feelings that they are holding down and suppressing, and they choose not to release them. So they need to experience this denseness of what they have done. In their ignorance, they need to experience the trauma of seeing their loved ones depart, and they need to experience damage that they have done to this Earth, and all the money that they thought they needed, and the ego was nothing. It means nothing, and they need to feel this denseness in their heart.

J: Thank you so much. I do appreciate that. Okay, and so then next, Subconscious, what is New Earth?

S: New Earth is a new beginning. New Earth is a new adventure. New Earth is pure light, pure joy, pure love, pure everything. There is no density allowed on New Earth. It is pure love. They will find their peace, their inner peace. It is being prepared. There are already people on there, but the main people will come. They are so excited to prepare it for their new people that will come. There are the trees; they have arrived—the butterflies, the dragonflies, the pets. They are all waiting there for everybody to come. It's going to be so, so magical. It is going to be a wonderful home for so many people, and they are going to be so proud of themselves for what they have experienced in the 3D. They will look back and laugh at what they went through, and they will see all the people that they have known over many lifetimes and for many planets. They are there waiting to celebrate with them together.

J: Wonderful, thank you so much, and if you had to describe physically what New Earth is, what would you say to us?

S: New Earth is a wonderful planet in the hidden solar system. This is being kept a secret. It's a wonderful secret. New Earth is full of vibrant colors and waterfalls and just pure air, pure love, and pure joy. It has been hidden from many for a very long time and very, very few people know where it is. It is a beautiful hidden secret, but it is there, and it is waiting.

J: Why does it have to be such a secret?

S: This has been kept a secret for many, many, many, many millenniums. This has been kept because it has been intercepted and has been moved many times. It has been intercepted by deceptive, deceptive people. We have sent some ships out to collect some people to take them to New Earth, but they have been intercepted. So this has to be kept a secret because we need it to be kept a secret for when the larger ships will come towards us on New Earth. They can arrive safely, and they will be protected the whole way. Many do not know the location of New Earth, and every time we are intercepted, we will move it slightly or hide it into another solar system, but it is always there, waiting.

J: Fantastic, are you able to give the vehicle a sneak peek of seeing or sensing the New Earth, please?

S: Yes, we can do that.

J: Wonderful, can you tell me what she is noticing?

S: She is feeling so elated. She can hardly take the pure love that's there—the lightness, the lightness of being, and the colors are so, so vibrant, and everybody's so, so equal, and everybody is loved and accepted, and... Oh, the lightness! The lightness of being, and the pureness of the air, and the wind in the trees, and the many, many birds singing. It's just pure joy. It's the moment when you sleep at night in the 3D, and you imagine that wonderful place where you go. You can smile to yourself and feel so at peace. This is the place that you have been seeing. This is not just a dream. This exists, and this is where many of you will go. It will be pure energy and light, and then truly magical and amazing. You need to focus on this, because it is not just a dream. This truly does exist, and we give you these pictures in your dream so you can experience it, and feel joy, and lift yourself from the 3D denseness, and know that it's coming. It's coming so soon, and you are going to love it so, so much.

J: Thank you, Subconscious. Is the vehicle herself going to the New Earth after the shift?

S: She has no time to go. She was due to go there, but she has urgent matters to attend to, so she will just be waving as she goes by and sending her love.

J: Okay, and do you want to give us insights into what she's going to be doing instead of the New Earth experience?

S: She has got a new planetary alignment to go to, and she has much negotiations to sort out. We are all awaiting her. We are all awaiting her and very excited for her arrival, and many like her. She was due to go to New Earth, but when she was due to shift earlier. But as she did not shift, there is no time to go to New Earth. She will be going to her planet, where we have been awaiting her again. She has much to do.

J: Thank you so much. I do understand that. Can you give me a sense of how people travel to the New Earth, please?

S: They will be traveling many ways. Some have a direct tunnel which is of pure light, and it is like a fast track. They go through, and they do their life review. They are purged as they travel. It's like a vortex, but it is full of pure white light. There are some that will go on small ships of two or three, that will be taken. This is not a direct route. As it could be intercepted, they are taking a roundabout route to get there so they cannot be detected. And our larger ships are there. They are in place. They are ready to take lots more—the people that will leave 3D. Their frequency codes will be heard, and they will match up with the ships, and they will be collected. Their body will be taken with them, but they will not be walking up the steps. They will be drifting up. They will feel at ease because their frequency codes will recognize that it's their feeling of home, and they will willingly go on to the ships. And they will be on there, and they will be processed on there, and helped from many different beings that are on there, waiting, ready. They will help them purge and go through the different sections that they need to on the ships, to cleanse before they arrive on the New Earth. Some will not go to the New Earth. They will be taken somewhere else on the ship.

J: Thank you, so they will take their full carbon-based bodies with them?

S: Some will do, yes, and some will not take their bodies with them.

J: What's the significance and purpose of taking their carbon-based bodies with them?

S: It is an agreement that they have made so they can recognize each other as they have not been processed. The sense of being processed is they have not fully purged their pain and density. So when they have done this, and they are cleansed, and feel pure joy and love in their heart, then the carbon-based body will be removed, and they will be pure light, ready to move to New Earth.

J: I see, yes, I do understand. So for those people who don't take their bodies, what's the purpose of that?

S: The people that do not take their bodies with them, they will be fast-tracked through, or they will be on the smaller ships, because they do not need to take their bodies with them.

J: Fascinating, and so what's going to happen to the vehicle? What is going to happen for her?

S: She is going to be fast-tracked, but as she does not do things by half as normal, she will be fast-tracked, and it will be diverted past New Earth.

J: I understand, okay, thank you. Could someone take a carbon-based body to go to the New Earth and be on the New Earth in a carbon-based body?

S: Yes.

J: Tell me about that.

S: This is part of their contract. This is to help people when they arrive, but they will not be there in the carbon-based body for long, as they will turn into pure light. They will not be able to hold on to their carbon-based body, and it is of no use there. They are there to greet people, to start when the big shift happens, when the larger ships arrive. They are there to greet, to make them feel at ease before the transition.

J: I see, and so would that be for everyone or just some?

S: Everyone.

J: Okay, and tell me more about how people find themselves arriving on the New Earth?

S: Some will arrive and be very confused, and feel as if they are in a dream, but when they see people that they recognize from the past—people that have passed, that come to greet them in their carbon-based bodies—they will be able to be told from them that they are now on New Earth, and it will be a smoother transition for them to understand.

J: Will it be their physical carbon-based bodies or will it be an illusion of the carbon-based bodies—a likeness, a look of a likeness?

S: This will be an illusion.

J: So they will be representing themselves as if they are in their carbon-based bodies?

S: Yes.

J: Okay, but the physical body, say for example that the vehicle is in now, could that be taken to the New Earth, as it is now?

S: She is not going to the New Earth.

J: So someone who is going to the New Earth, could they physically take their physical bodies that they're living in now, directly as is, and go to the New Earth, and be on the New Earth?

S: As will also be transmuted into an illusion.

J: Okay, all right, I guess we get a bit hung up over the names of carbon-based bodies versus the illusion of the carbon-based bodies versus the physicality of what we understand the carbon-based body to be.

S: This is correct.

J: Thank you. Okay, what point do people move into their crystalline-based bodies? How does that actually occur?

S: This happens on the ships. There are three parts to the ship. There is the arrival lounge that they will be in and greeted, and then they will go through the process of letting go of the density. They will be helped to overcome any fear or any doubt or any worry. When they find their inner love and their inner peace—sometimes the work that they have not done in the 3D—and they feel pure light, then they will transition to the third stage where they are just the illusion before they land on New Earth.

J: Thank you. Can you tell me about what we call the crystalline-based bodies, our light bodies? What's going on there? How does it feel to be one of those?

S: This is the magical feeling where, you feel the example we are giving, is where you feel total lightness just before you drift off to sleep, and you can't feel your body. It feels as if you're floating on the cloud just as your head hits the pillow, and it just dissolves into the pillow. This is the lightness. This is where when you sleep at night, we come and send you updates and upgrades. This is pure energy that we are going through, and we check anything that needs healing. This makes you one and makes you feel so light. It is a lightness. It is a light code that enwraps you, and everybody has their own light code enwrapment that is around them. This is what is recognized on the ships, and this is how people recognize each other when they go through the three stages.

J: Thank you so much. I really appreciate that clarification, thank you. Subconscious, in terms of people talking about the New Earth being here now and that they are in the fifth dimension, where are they getting their information from?

S: This is from people that claim they are light workers, because people have forgotten who they are. People are trying desperately to find connection, and people are not listening to their own inner moral compasses. They are feeling they need to follow people that say they know what they are talking about, because they have massive egos. People are not listening to their own inner moral compass. People inside really do know that this is not the 5D, but they are very influenced because they have lost their own minds, and they are being influenced by other people.

J: Okay, when the shift does happen, and people do find themselves in the fifth dimension, will they notice?

S: They will notice. Some will fight this, because some are going to stay in the 3D on the Old Earth with the rest. Yes, they will notice.

J: Okay, and from your perspective, Subconscious, when could we start officially labeling this planet "the Old Earth"?

S: This has already started.

J: Okay, thank you. Thank you so much. Is there any other information you'd like us to know today?

S: The Earth is tilting back on its axis, and Gaia has left. This has left a wash of events. There are many events that are happening on this Old Earth planet. We like people to know to hold the faith and hope and remember who they really are inside, and to have no fear, and to trust we are there with them. We feel their pain, but we are sending so much love to all of you, and to never forget you are never ever alone.

Session 6

J: I'd like to call upon the Subconscious please.

P: Alright.

J: Okay, thank you, are you able to do a body scan for her body, and tell me what is happening to her?

P: Yes, just a second. There seems to be a blue light at the bottom of the feet.

J: Can you tell me about that blue light please?

P: It just seems to be there. It seems to be staying there.

J: Okay, thank you. In terms of her body, is there anything that you can heal or balance or that needs to be addressed and sorted out?

P: There is a renewal, like Spring, generating itself from the heart outward.

J: Well, that sounds like fantastic news, that is wonderful. Can you explain to me some of her aches and pains? What's going on there for her body?

P: The shoulder where she's feeling pain is experiencing light. But it's a different light that's at the foot. It's a white and yellow light. It's part of the renewal. The fact that there is pain that is symptomatic of having a body that exists on this planet. It's kind of part of the experience. If she's worried about it, it's not necessarily anything to worry about. It's part of life as walking along this Earth plane.

J: Okay, well, thank you. She did say that she wanted to be able to understand more about the right shoulder. She did know and state that there was an attachment to the right shoulder that was giving her discomfort. How can you explain to me about this attachment, please, Subconscious?

P: The attachment grew there from an early experience that she had as a child, and it became part of a belief system. And what it allowed for was for her to further explore and understand the dynamics of the way that we interact with each other on this Earth. There is the dynamic of a parent who is in a leadership role and has domination over a child, and it precipitates a way of dealing with the world. And what this did for her was it made her feel responsible to take upon herself the burdens of others, and she was allowed to feel the weight of what it is to carry the burdens of others. To do this helped her understand the dynamics of love and what happens when you take on a burden, and it becomes very, very heavy. There is a point where you need to allow that burden to be shared. Or understand that taking on too much of a burden is no longer helpful for the person for whom you're taking on the burden. It's a very effective way to learn human interaction, human dynamics, human relationships, and interpersonal skills. It is that, but it was a tiny little root that grew into a large burden upon her. No, not a burden, it was a...it's like a growth that was on the shoulder. It has been removed. It is no longer there. The root is gone, the effects are gone. The shoulder itself now is clear of all those burdens. This is something that she can understand, going forward this is no longer necessary for her to operate under. She can go forward without shouldering so many burdens for other people. She understands that better.

J: Thank you. So, instead of it being an entity or an attachment as such, it's really a connection to reminding her what is her responsibilities and what's not her responsibilities?

P: Yes.

J: Okay, thank you for helping me understand that. So that would be fantastic if you could release the sensations of that discomfort for her. Are there any other discomforts in her body that you would like to help assist with today?

P: She is experiencing some discomfort in her lower back and the light will go there.

J: Okay, well, thank you so much. I really would appreciate you giving her a beautiful healing and balancing of anything she needs to be healed and balanced throughout the session. If there is anything you need me to understand to be able to help learn the significance and purpose of certain things that are happening to her body, I would really appreciate it if you could share that with me. And let me know if there is anything else you'd like to discuss before we start doing these questions today.

P: We can proceed.

J: Thank you so much, Subconscious. I deeply appreciate that. So, out of curiosity, what dimension are you in, Subconscious?

P: 5th.

J: Thank you so much, and from your perspective, in terms of what we call the 'shift', what does 'shifting to 5D' mean for humanity?

P: The way that I perceive it is: dropping of the trappings of mortality and becoming crystalline. It happens to look like a lighter, brighter body. It is a lighter and brighter existence. There is far less density, and that means that this enables connections and love and joy can flow. Whereas, when the bodies, the heavy dense bodies, that exist on this Earth, the barriers will be eliminated. There's so much light that will be able to penetrate and flow and unify the souls. You're currently so very individualized within bodies. The understanding and the awareness will be enhanced.

J: Fantastic, thank you. So, it sounds like it's a physical shift?

P: Absolutely, it's a physical shift. The physicality of the human body will remain here, upon this Earth. And the actual spirits, the essence— will move, shift, be transferred, to an entirely new area, plane, dimension, This is not where people will be staying. It won't be here, upon this planet Earth. It will be, it will be shifted, shifted. Yes, the word 'shift'. That's it, it's exactly what's happening, being moved.

J: Thank you so much, and Subconscious, are you able to explain to me the life contract of this planet's soul in terms of 'shifting to 5D'? What does that mean?

P: The soul of the planet has experienced so much. All that needed to be experienced, more than perhaps needed to be experienced to be able to go to the next or to, we'll say ascend, ascend to the next experience. The soul of the planet has been through incredible experiences, challenging experiences, and it is fully prepared for the next step in the ascension.

J: Thank you, and in terms of the Old Earth, what is that referring to, the Old Earth?

P: Maybe one could envision it as understanding what it is to see deaths. The body remains behind, spirit moves on. There is a vessel that is no longer needed or is being utilized. The essence of that is now free to become a new creation, in a very new and elevated sense. Retaining all the experience, the knowledge, everything—it is essential that remains with the spirit, while the physical body, the denser matter is left behind.

J: Thank you so much and Subconscious, I know there could be many purposes for those life lessons to have the experience of the Old Earth, but could you explain to me some of the reasons why some people would like to experience the Old Earth, please?

P: There seems to be in certain individual souls an absolute insatiable curiosity that, what could something that they have perhaps not experienced before, what would that look like, how would I feel? Curiosity is seductive and it can propel certain souls to tread where their eyes are dark and it's difficult and you know a path that another soul will never consider. There is just a need to know, they want to feel it, they want to see it, share it. They're brave souls.

J: Thank you, I love that, it's all purposeful, I get it. Thank you. So then, Subconscious, can you explain to me what the New Earth is then, please?

P: What the New Earth is?

the SHIFT to NEW EARTH

J: Yes, we hear this term often, so I'm curious, what is the New Earth?

P: The way that it appears is it looks bright, round, crystalline, shimmering. It appears to be so much bigger than what the physical planet Earth is. It's like it's permeable. When a human understands the planet Earth that revolves around the sun, it's crusty, it's dense, it has weight, it has mass, it has structure. However, the New Earth has almost transparency, like the bodies of the inhabitants, they will be able to move in and out and the New Earth will be able to... how about the word respirate, maybe we could use a word respirate, just permeable, breathes, the spirit moves, the energy moves. The restrictions that are experienced on the physical planet Earth are no longer there. There is an existence that is so free and so vibrant. There is a sense of purity, there is a sense of joy, there is no darkness. There's a perception of darkness on the planet Earth; there is no darkness on the New Earth.

J: Thank you, and so in terms of our current bodies, you're suggesting that we can't take our current bodies to the New Earth?

P: Why would anyone want to continue to exist in the form of a dense body that is limited by the conditions that exist in a third dimensional framework? Why would you choose that? It is completely unnecessary. There is absolutely no reason to continue to live in the human form that exists on the planet Earth, in a fifth dimensional space. It would feel like a cold, dark, clammy prison, when you can have a body that is full of light.

J: Okay, thank you. I understand and so the New Earth is a fifth dimensional planet which is completely separate from this planet we're currently living on now. Is that how you want me to understand this?

P: This is how it is perceived, yes. There is a separation. There is a definite dimensional difference, it is distinctively different.

J: So there is a 3D planet, and then there is a 5D planet?

P: Yes there is.

J: And the soul from this current planet that we're living in, in the 3D, how does it get to the other planet in 5D?

P: The soul of this planet is there. There is a small, small fraction of that soul here, and here there is a link, and there will come a time with that link when all the energy that belongs to the beautiful soul will be extracted from the physical 3D Earth, for all of that energy to be on the New Earth.

J: Okay, thank you so much. Subconscious, can you please give the vehicle a sense of her arriving on the New

Earth and what can she see when she's having a look and a peek at the New Earth?

P: There will be a sense of music, not music that's understood by the physical ears, but in music that is heard in every aspect of the being. That's the music that comes from people living as they were intended to live in beauty and harmony, existing within a chorus. It's so beautiful. The music may be the first thing she notices.

J: And what will she see or sense when she arrives on the New Earth?

P: Perhaps it'll be the colors, the iridescent colors. If you could imagine the iridescence looks like soap bubbles, floating in the air, how it moves. It sparkles, and you can see colors moving. The senses of a fifth dimensional being, observe and feel and interact so differently than what they do in this density. So the experiences are difficult to make analogies from, from this physical plane into that plane. But if you can imagine the colors that are iridescent, moving, they interplay because there's light everywhere. The light goes in and out of the colors and then there's music. The music plays, music doesn't play—it exists! The music exists on its own, it is a part of that dimension. It is not separate, it is not something that somebody puts their hand to or their voice to—the music exists. So perhaps it's the music, perhaps it's the colors that may be noticed.

J: Thank you. Can you give her that sense of being on the New Earth now, and how will she notice and feel about that?

P: Incredible, ecstatic, coming from a sense of doom into a new way of feeling.

J: Could it be said, Subconscious, that she's always been searching and longing for that frequency of the fifth dimension?

P: Absolutely, she's been searching for that. She has not found it here. She has not found it anywhere here. It has not been found here, and yet, she is deeply longing for it. Emotionally, she is so hungry for it. Yes, she has.

J: Thank you, and we were talking earlier about her liking me to ask you if you can help her with her sugar cravings. Would this now be able to help her heal that inner child, knowing that she is going to find what she's always been searching for her entire life: that sweetness, that joy that is in the fifth dimension?

P: Yes

J: Is there anything else you would like us to understand about her sugar addiction?

P: Her sugar addiction is a manifestation of exactly as you described it, as the feeling of ingesting sugar is replacing the longing for the connection. It has soothed feelings of abandonment. It has soothed death. It has soothed those feelings for her, and she will soon understand those cravings.

J: Thank you. Subconscious, are you able to balance her gut bacteria, please, to be able to help her not crave that sugar as much? Would that help at all?

P: That is definitely something that can be done, yes. I perceive at this moment that the springtime garden that is growing within her is now growing within the digestive area, and there is balance there. There is an appropriate balance.

J: Okay, so how will she feel after this session? Will she still have those cravings?

P: No, not at all.

J: What would you like her to replace for her diet? Is there anything she's lacking in her diet that you would like her to start eating more of?

P: Green, green, green—if it's green, it will provide rich nutrition. Light things that are not heavy. Anything that is associated with an animal product, let's perhaps avoid..

J: Why is it that some people can eat animal products and some people can't?

P: The vibration. It's a choice of vibration. If an animal product is ingested into the body, it brings a certain vibration with it. It interacts with the body, and it's a denser interaction with the physical body. And because the human has and is experiencing the physical form taking in an animal product, meat perhaps, interacts in a denser form. If a lighter feeling is desired, then a lighter food brings a lighter and finer vibration to the body. If a choice is made, you will feel it in your body. If it feels appropriate, if it feels necessary, then seek after that vibration. However, for her body, it would be advisable to avoid that denser, heavier intake.

J: Thank you very much, Subconscious. Now, finally, we hear many people talking about the New Earth being here now, being this planet, and that we are in the fifth dimension. Where are they getting this information from?

P: It would appear that information that would suggest that the New Earth was developing here, right here on this third dimensional planet. But what I'm seeing, is it would exist in the mindset of an individual who perhaps was feeling the ascension process unfolding within their own body. And they feel that that is what's happening to the Earth. That is a perception that is limited to the person's experience, their own personal journey of enlightenment. However, if someone feels that way, they need to continue to understand, to see what else is happening. But the idea that the New Earth is here—it's not, it's not. The human mind struggles to clearly understand many different concepts. It is not unusual at all to have the human mind be confused or misunderstand or fabricate. There will come a point in time where all will understand exactly what is happening and will be able to freely, clearly, thoroughly understand the dynamics. Everyone's journey takes its own course.

J: Thank you, is there any other information you would like to share with us today?

P: This is me again, this is me coming through. There's something going on with my foot. I don't understand what it is.

J: Okay, so just relax, and we can ask the Subconscious about that. So just enjoy the way it feels to have deep relaxation moving through the body, and as we ask the Subconscious to return, we would like to know what is happening to the foot please?

P: There is some resistance in her right foot. The blue light that is at her foot and her feet would like to enter in, and the foot, the right foot, is resisting.

J: Subconscious, does that blue light have a message for her?

P: The blue light would like to direct her, the blue light would like to illuminate the steps which she is taking. The foot was recently touched and healed by the hand of Jesus, and she seems to be blocking the path for that light to be able to enter into that foot. Despite the healing, there's a blockage.

J: And when did that blockage occur?

P: It appears that it has entered there recently.

J: And the purpose of it being there, what would you like her to understand?

P: She can ask for it to be removed, she needs to ask for it to be removed. She needs to take the initiative and ask for it to be removed. Like she took the initiative to ask for the shoulder to be healed, she needs to take the initiative and ask for this blockage to be healed. The left foot is fine, it appears clear. In the right foot there's blockage.

J: And the significance of that blockage is?

P: It's more programming. It is very similar to the programming that was causing the growth, or however you want to describe it, that was on the shoulder. It is made of the same material. It has lodged itself into the foot. It can be seen clearly. She can be responsible for removing it. She can take the initiative. She can understand how to do that, and she will benefit from the process of doing it. It has been started with the healing that was given by her understanding of Jesus, and now she can learn to do the next step. She understands. Now that she knows it's there, she can do it.

J: How fantastic, thank you. Thank you for helping her to be guided to be able to empower herself through this. I really appreciate that. Subconscious, are there any more messages you have for us today?

P: Be joyful, be joyful, there is so much to be joyful for. It is a time to rejoice that the transition is happening. Be joyful.

J: I think she'll be able to do that really well. Thank you so much, Subconscious, I really appreciate all the information and healing you've provided for her today. When she goes back through this material and puts it into place, how will she feel within herself?

P: There is a sense of balance, and we will leave her with a sense of springtime.

J: Such a beautiful sense, thank you. Is there any other information you would like to discuss?

P: Her upcoming trip with her daughter will be wonderful. There will be a special bond between her and her daughter. She will understand so much more of what their mission is together. They are bringing much joy in.

She needs to be sure to touch the ground, touch the ground, be sure to touch the Earth, touch the Earth. Profoundly important to touch the Earth. That is all.

J: Much appreciated, thank you, Subconscious, for all that you have been able to do for her and for us all. So we'll ask you to recede to where you belong.

the SHIFT to NEW EARTH

Session 7

J: I'd like to call upon the Subconscious, please. Thank you. Are you able to do a body scan, and see what's happening to her body, please?

N: Yes, she seems to be fine, it's just muscles as she needs to move a little bit more. She just needs to stretch, do yoga, and walk a bit more. Everything else is good.

J: Fantastic.

N: Her shoulder, like she mentioned.

J: Do you want to remind her of the discomfort of that right shoulder? What's going on there for her?

N: She's doing way too much. She's doing everything. She works at home, so she feels like she has to do everything. She doesn't have to, she just has to ask. She'll be fine with that. She's got it figured out.

J: Thank you. What else about her body? Is every system in her body balanced and harmonized?

N: She's going through a scan right now, just to check. Okay, yep, everything's good.

J: Fantastic! Thank you. Are you able to give her beautiful, uplifting, healing energy while we continue on with the session today?

N: Yes.

J: Thank you, lovely. Subconscious, what dimension are you in?

N: Arcturian, in the ninth dimension.

J: Thank you so much, I do appreciate that. Lovely to talk to you again, Arcturian. From your perspective, in terms of the shift, what does shifting to 5D mean for humanity?

N: A lot of people think it's just changing your mindset on this planet, but there's more to it. You have to be ready to ascend to this shift. Not everybody's meant to do this big shift. Some people's lessons are done and they're meant to shift over. That's when their vehicle expires here in this lifetime and their soul can ascend.

J: Can you tell us what ascending means, then? What does that actually look like?

N: Your body has to expire here. It's just a vehicle, so it has to expire. It is going to look like death to other people, but your soul just keeps going. The soul's been through this so many times already, they've just forgotten. Once they expire here, then they evolve and move to where they're supposed to go. Everyone is meant to go to different places. Not everybody's shifting in the same direction. Some people are meant to go to New Earth, and some people aren't ready yet. It's not a punishment. It just depends where you are with your life lessons at the time of the shift.

J: Thank you so much. What is the life contract for this planet, for the soul of this planet, in terms of shifting to 5D? How can you explain to us the life contract of this planet's soul?

N: I feel like this planet doesn't have that soul anymore. I feel like she's moved on already. She's attached by a cord, but she's not fully here now. That's why the planet and the humans are going through all this purging.

J: So, she's left the 3D and is she going to the fifth dimension?

N: Yes, she's already there.

J: What does that look like for her?

N: It's peaceful, and it's more beautiful. There's more balance, and she's not being taken advantage of in the same way she was here. She's respected and everything's in balance. Things are not perfect, but they are way better for her than her situation on this Earth. Everything surrounding her has more of a respect towards her and an understanding. Maybe more so because everybody's telepathically able to communicate, so everything's all in the open. They can all communicate with her openly there, so it's a lot easier that way. She's not being taken advantage of or being destroyed.

J: Fantastic, thank you. That is wonderful! What is the term Old Earth referring to?

N: The Old Earth would be the "label" for this planet after the shift. There will be different shifts, because it looks different to everybody. Again, it comes back to perspective, some people see it as everybody's dying. Everything's going to be in turmoil. Everything's getting flipped upside down. But, the ones that know about this and are expecting it, they will see it differently. They'll see it as more of a celebration. It just depends how you're going to view it.

J: So that's still a future experience for humanity, then?

N: Definitely.

J: Thank you. Subconscious, would you give us a sense of what event or events would have to take place, that we could understand, that we could then start calling this Earth 'Old Earth'?

N: It depends, as everyone's label is different for that. Some people call it 'Old Earth' right away when they see something big is happening, and other people won't relate to that at all. It depends where you live on this planet. Some people will see the light from a "solar flash" and some people won't see it. Some people just hear about it. Some people will see a volcano, some people will see and feel an earthquake. So, it just depends on your perspective.

J: Thank you. That makes sense. While there would be a huge range of lessons to be learned on the Old Earth, why would certain people want to experience the Old Earth? What are the lessons they're seeking?

N: It's like their soul needs to live through that experience to understand. Some people, or souls, had an experience here on Earth and they've experienced similarities throughout other lifetimes, but they still haven't learned the lesson—to totally follow their intuition, as opposed to following the crowd. By always following others, you're not learning, growing, or moving forward. So, they will be "left behind" on Old Earth because they need to see and experience it for themselves. They need to see that big ending, to be caught in that moment, so they will have no choice but to reflect within at that point. They will have nobody else there to follow online or on TV. They're there to focus on themselves; just to be with themselves and to go within and find all the right answers and everything that's most purposeful for them.

the SHIFT to NEW EARTH

J: Thank you. Subconscious, can you tell me what New Earth is?

N: It's a different place altogether. It has nothing at all to do with this place, here. It's a whole, new, different place. The location can't be said out loud. If we tell you today, the information will be out there and it can be jeopardized. So, the less information about the location, the better, but it's a totally different place. It's not here. This planet here has gone through so much. Humanity has taken advantage of it, shit on it, destroyed it, and poisoned it. It's so bad that it needs to clean itself out. It needs to go through fire, ice, wind, through all the changes to cleanse from top to bottom. So, the ones that think staying on this Earth and fixing it to have a better life are misinformed. You cannot fix all that. It would take even longer than humanity can even imagine. They would have to go through so much turmoil of deep fires and deep ice ages. You cannot survive that, even if you went deep, deep, deep into the middle of the Earth. There are caves there already that need fixing. There is nowhere else to go. This whole planet needs to be purged completely, and rebirthed completely, before humanity can come back here and have an existence on it to begin with. So, to go to 5D is a totally different place. Sure, you could start doing your inner work and empowering yourself and growing closer to 5D thinking—but only to a certain point. The 3D energy is so dense. As much as the most perfect souls are trying to make their way to 5D, the density here on Earth still breaks them down. It's a totally different location.

J: Thank you so much. Are you able to give the vehicle a peek at the New Earth then can you tell me what she would be noticing first as she sees the New Earth?

N: The colors are different—it's more vibrant. Even the sky is not just one color. Here we see blue, gray and white clouds, but the sky there will be like purples and teals. The colors! She notices the colors right away, just shining so vibrantly.

J: What would she be noticing about herself?

N: She's so much lighter, so much lighter, and able to shift a little bit to change the way she looks. It's not instant, like a magician waving a wand. It will be learning to slowly transform your looks. For example, you can slowly learn to transform your hair color or tighten your skin, so you can look how you prefer to look. It's all done with love. When you give love and intention to everything, all will work together and benefit each soul.

J: Wonderful! Thank you so much. Subconscious, while I asked for a body scan for the vehicle, I didn't realize there was another being in the room. Can you tell me if we can help that dog? It seems like the dog would potentially like some attention. Could you do a body scan for the dog and tell me what's happening for that dog please?

N: The dog has anxiety. The dog cannot be away from this vehicle. The vehicle is trying really hard to teach the dog distance and peace and love. She even went out and got the poor thing a crate yesterday, just so he can have his own safe space and hopefully understand that he can't be with her all the time.

J: Subconscious, what is the life contract between the vehicle and the dog, please?

N: He's always been around her, always. He's just supposed to be with her. She left him in another life. His anxiety is about being abandoned, and he doesn't like that. He's here to learn how to be alone a little bit. Poor dog.

J: So, can we reassure him that he's not really going to be left alone this lifetime? Now that she knows that, can she support him and support his anxiety? What else can we do?

N: Yes, we can put a light around him and make him feel safe. He just doesn't feel safe.

J: What happened to him when she left him in that other lifetime?

N: He was left completely alone. It caught him by surprise. He was also an animal in that lifetime. He was her pet then, just like today.

J: Okay. Can we send love, protection and support for that animal that was alone, trusting that it was purposeful to learn self-empowerment? May that heal and release the anxiety from this dog in this lifetime. Is that appropriate?

N: Yes, and thank you. It will really benefit them both. Thank you!

J: Bless them both. Thank you so much! Okay, getting back to the questions. Subconscious, can we take our current bodies to the New Earth?

N: Yes, some will. It's not for everybody.

J: Tell me about those who can take their bodies to the New Earth. What does that look like or how does that occur?

N: I almost feel like they'll get activated at the right time, or they could just astral travel.

J: I see.

N: Some people can do that in their sleep right now. So, if you're able to do that in your sleep right now—just a second—*it won't be the same body*. It's not the same dense body. It's your soul. Your soul has to disconnect from your body.

J: Okay. Let me ask again to clarify. Will we be able to take our current bodies to New Earth?

N: No, *not the physical body itself*. No, it won't make it. The body itself is too dense to do that. You would have to go through so much to make that happen. Only the soul, just like astral traveling, but not the body itself.

J: Okay, yes. I guess if people are trying to read the energy of themselves, being here and then on the New Earth, you're potentially reading the signature of the soul versus the signature frequency of the body. Could that be how people get a bit confused seeing themselves on the New Earth?

N: You could see yourself on New Earth and imagine yourself.

J: Can you place the vehicle on the New Earth now, and tell me what she's noticing about her physical body on the New Earth?

N: Yes. Everything's better, with more flexibility. This body is the ideal type that her soul feels most comfortable in. But again, each soul is very different, so you can manifest whatever look feels more comfortable

the SHIFT to NEW EARTH

to you. So some people, or souls, will come across as something a little different than others, but their looks won't shock one another. Once you're there, you don't have that judgment. It's the feeling that all is well, and as it should be. So, in this lifetime here today, this vehicle feels like she got cheated. She didn't get enough hair for a hairdresser. She feels she should have gotten way more hair. So, on New Earth, she sees herself with way more hair.

J: Sort of like a sasquatch[17]?

N: (hearty laughter) That's awesome! That's funny because the vehicle's family saw a sasquatch yesterday, so it's awesome you said that!

J: When you give her the sense of being on the New Earth, how does she feel about being there?

N: It's more relaxed and laid back. There's more acceptance. There are beautiful colors. You don't have to eat the same way. You don't have to travel the same way. Everything's easier. You don't have the same health problems. It's still not perfect or like heaven. It's not like once you get there, all your problems are done and all your life lessons are over. You're still there to learn and grow. You're still there to go through lessons and find

---

[17] Original humans without any DNA upgrades.

purposes. Some people see it as like heaven on Earth or heaven and you're "done." It's never done.

J: Can you tell me some of the things that would be perceived as problems on the New Earth?

N: Creating, because you're going to be creating everything. For example, here you can just go to a hardware store and pick up all your wood and start building. But, on the New Earth, you don't have a hardware store. You have to create with your imagination. It will be trial and error to try and create something in front of you. Let's say you want to build a cabin, so you have to imagine all the lumber being put together. You have to imagine all of it being like "Lego" pieces being put together. But it takes practice to "build" your first thing. It's like building a house here. The first time you build a house, it's going to be a shitty house, especially if you have no guidance and no help. As you keep building more houses, you learn from experience. So, because you don't have the experience of using your imagination to create, it'll just take time and practice to learn. It'll be frustrating at first if you're not patient.

J: I see. It is fascinating, thank you. I could see the struggles there, but it's very motivating to be able to sort of master that at the same time too.

N: You're even going to need to use your imagination to create food. Food will grow everywhere, but you still have to create your gardens. You still have to work on "your" land. It's not your land, it's everyone's land, shared equally. We have to put love into it. But people will be frustrated because you can't just learn how to do that overnight. It's a skill that comes with time.

J: Are those the sort of skill sets that people are starting to learn now, on this planet?

N: Not truly the same, but similar. This planet here is all about using tools and equipment. You won't really need tools and equipment, you just need an imagination on New Earth.

J: Thank you so much. Can someone in a carbon-based body be on the New Earth or any 5D planet? We also refer to the bodies on the New Earth as crystalline. We don't quite know all of the matter that creates these bodies that we can project on the New Earth. Can you help me understand about the differences between the bodies we have here now, on this planet, versus the bodies we will have on the New Earth?

N: The bodies you have here, they take a lot of work. They're very dense. You get what you put in, but everything's physical. On New Earth, you can just create what you look like. It comes down to your imagination. Again, you have to imagine how you want to look, what you want to project, and as you practice projecting, you'll succeed. But here, you can't just imagine and then manifest your skin or long, thick hair. On the New Earth, you can't just do that immediately either. It takes practice, but it's the way it works.

J: Just so I understand, the body on the New Earth, what is it made of? Humans are sort of fixated with labels about carbon and crystalline, but how can you explain the physical or the non-physical bodies that are on the New Earth?

N: I'm not getting anything.

J: That's okay, it's fine. They're just details, and it's not really that significant. We'll find out when we shift. It is quite complicated when we ask about the molecular composition of our bodies, so thank you. Subconscious, we hear from many other people talking about the New Earth being here now, on this planet, and that we are in the fifth dimension. Where are they getting the information from?

N: It's from the ego. That's what the ego wants because it's more comfortable. It's threatened by the thought of losing this 3D body. It's protecting itself. Some egos can't accept that, so many people will "die," not understanding or accepting the truth or purpose. Also, how would so many people react to hearing that all at the same time? You can tell people the truth, and they don't want to hear it, because they haven't done the inner work to understand. Believing that we're already in 5D makes the ego more comfortable.

J: Why do you think people still use the ego to talk about metaphysics?

N: Because they can't tap in. They won't go inward and connect with their teams. They can't hear them, so they make it up. They make up what's comfortable.

J: Is it challenging for subconsciouses and guides to have your 3D counterparts not listening to the information you're trying to provide to people?

N: Yes, extremely. We have to lower our vibration and meet them halfway, but they have to raise their vibration to meet us there. If they can't raise their vibration to meet us halfway, they can't connect. It's very frustrating, because we're here for them all the time, and we want them to connect. We see them trying, and we realize how dense it is, so dense, that they're having a hard time raising their vibration. They have all the tools in front of them, and they know how to make it work. They're just frustrated. It's easier to give in, and then their ego wins.

J: I see. So, what sort of events would need to take place before the shifts? For example, are there any human actions or experiences that aren't natural disasters?

N: Yes, especially when you look at this vaccine that's going on right now. Many people had to go through that experience just to know that they're putting all their trust in the wrong people. So, they're going to have big epiphanies when they realize that all the trust they had in, for example, big pharma or media, was misplaced. That's going to be a huge lesson right there all on its own. But again, that only refers to a certain percentage of people, not everybody got vaccinated. There's just one scenario right there. We all need to live certain lessons, and the lessons have to be completed. We can't just end things too quickly because they're all here to fulfill their contracts. They all have their lessons to learn. Some of them have lessons relating to family. Family dynamics provide huge lessons. People on this Earth planet have been brainwashed into thinking families are everything and that your family's supposed to be their rock. Many families, however, are dysfunctional. Families exist here to make you see, grow and evolve. You're not supposed to stick around. You're supposed to move, to see, to have adventures. Some families disempower you and are constantly holding you back. There are many events or holidays on the calendar where people feel obligated to get together with family. They do not need to keep attending these events. Once they learn they can detach and they're free, their families will not pull them down, and they'll have more experiences and lessons. Nobody's learning anything from staying put, or staying glued, to their families. So, between the vaccine lessons and letting go of family, and all of the programming, those are huge lessons they need to learn right now. People are being relocated for a reason, just to be able to disconnect from family. You're not supposed to stay put.

J: I could see that it would take quite a lot of courage for people to expand and empower themselves beyond their social systems or family. Thank you so much. Is there any other information you would like us to understand about the shift for humanity?

N: The shift is different for everybody. What some people are going to experience, other people won't. Again, it just depends on where you'll live on the planet. Geographically, it's all different. So, for example, the laser event. We keep seeing it being pushed. I can't really say if that's going to be happening or if it's something else. Let's say that does happen. A lot of people will see that as a shift, but some people won't see it at all. It just depends on your perspective. Did I answer your question, or did I get off track?

J: It's a big question, so I understand. It's difficult to be able to cover every aspect of it, so we understand. Thank you very much. Are there any other messages you would like us to know today?

N: You're doing a lot of good for humanity, Jo, and we thank you. This is going to help a lot of people understand and connect some dots. But we do see a lot of people aren't meant to get these messages at all. Even though we want everyone to hear it equally, it's only meant for certain ears. Some people will listen, but they will not put the pieces together the same way, and that's okay. It's not meant for them to go that way. It's almost like looking at a "w" and you have four people in a circle looking at the same "w." One person will say "no, that's a three." Another person will say "no, it's an 'm'." Another person will say "no, it's just mountains." It just depends where you're going to be, at the time, on how you perceive everything. It depends, but they need to learn it's going to be different for everybody. Thank you, Jo, because you are doing a lot of good and a lot of good people that do need to hear these messages are on top of it.

J: Well, thank you. Subconscious, I trust that all will be directed to these messages if they are appropriate for them. I trust that those people who cannot hear this information at this time will be protected away from this, because we know it can be quite triggering when you hear the truth about the shift.

N: Definitely. It's definitely a shift where you're relocating away from here. Nobody's coming back here for a very, very long time.

J: Thank you so much, Subconscious. How is her body feeling and how is the dog's body feeling?

N: She's feeling really relaxed. She's doing absolutely fantastic, and the dog seems to be doing better. He's just lonely, but he's fine.

J: We sent him a big love bubble and appreciation to allow this session to happen today, and are there any private messages that you want to share with the vehicle that doesn't get shared publicly?

N: She's doing exactly what she's supposed to do, and she's listening. We're really proud. She's helping a lot of people. Even though she's got cheeky comments and she comes off as being a little weird sometimes, she's got her humor to back her up, and we're right there cheering her on. She's doing fine.

J: I think she's doing great! She was mentioning her frustrations when she was giving clients incredible sessions, and they weren't listening to the session. Can we ask for all of the Subconsciouses from all of her clients to empower and inspire those clients enough to go and listen to the sessions that they've had with her? The information is profound, the healing is profound, and we are wishing for everyone to step up and face their concerns and fears, and listen to their sessions to empower themselves completely.

N: Yes, thank you.

J: Are there any other messages that the dog would like to share with us today?

N: The dog's frustrated. He just just wants to be by her side. He doesn't understand why she's trying to spend time away from him.

J: Are there any other messages you would like to share with us, Subconscious?

N: Everything's exactly how it's supposed to be. Just go with the flow, it's fine. Sometimes overthinking everything is too much, so we just have to "go with it." People are forgetting to have fun. They need to have fun, be silly, and let go a little bit. That would help so much. Everything's gotten so serious these last two years, more serious than ever. People really need to learn how to just let go, have fun, and laugh at themselves. It's so important.

J: Absolutely. Can we ask all the collectives to be able to help inspire many and all people to be able to find their fun again and to treat themselves to having fun, to empower themselves, and enjoy each moment that they have here on this planet at this time?

N: Yes, yes, yes.

J: Thank you so much.

Session 8

J: I'd like to call upon the Subconscious, please?

A: We are here.

J: Hello, again. May you do a body scan, and tell me what is happening to her body?

A: Yes, thank you. She feels really good and relaxed right now. She has conscious concerns still with back pain. It's, as she knows, it's muscle tightness, and she has listened to my sessions and there were videos about releasing the muscle tightness that she consciously tries to do, so that helps. She's having acupuncture. There's nothing physical, and again, this is something that will just take a little time to work through. It's a process, we'll admit/she'll let us admit, that it's something we talked about previously, that it goes back to the emotional carrying a heavy load. She recognizes that, and she's discussed that with her partner. He's receptive and understanding, and making his own efforts to do more of his part to help take some of the parts of 3D life, the financial part of that load, off of her. So that will help her, but it's not going to be immediate like, "Oh I feel better". It's a process, because it's multi-faceted. It's not only that emotional aspect that is causing this, it's also body mechanics. You know, it's just something that's got several aspects. Again we talk about getting a good pair of shoes to work in. She's of a certain age where prior wear and tear is more evident on her body. She's doing stretches and some yoga poses that really, really help, so it's just going to be a process. But as far as her body, that's really the only thing with her, that we'll continue to help her with. Everything else seems to be pretty well in alignment for her today at this point.

J: Thank you so much. Are you able to continually help her release any tensions anywhere in the body and be able to have a profound enjoyable healing session today?

A: Yes, yes, yes.

J: Thank you, I know she deserves a spa treatment, and I know you do such great work in releasing the tensions and any pressures that we have within our systems. Subconscious, can you help me understand what dimension you are in?

A: 11th.

J: Thank you so much, and from your perspective, Subconscious, in terms of the word "shift", what does shifting to 5D mean for humanity?

A: There's difficulty formulating words to adequately describe or express. Not that we're dumbing you down or that you wouldn't understand, but sometimes there's a communication gap. She's trying to come in and sort it out, but we're just gonna get to the crux of it, because you know English words can have so many different meanings in one single word. But as to what I believe you're asking, would you mind just repeating the question?

J: Sure, absolutely, and while I know she would love to answer this herself, we're asking the Subconscious today. We know it's a very broad question, and we trust that the most appropriate information that you give us, even though it's one aspect of a very complex situation, we trust that you will be able to give us the most appropriate information for us to learn from today.

A: I'm sorry to interrupt you, I apologize, but I recall the word relocation, "shift" equals relocation. It's a weird word that has been chosen because many schools of thought are amongst all of you on how and what this is. Some people will say the consciousness, yes the consciousness does need to be elevated in order to tolerate the relocation. "Shift" is a shitty word, sorry but shift is not, it's not a shift, it's a relocation. But there does have to be an elevation of consciousness to a higher vibration in order for you all to tolerate and survive. It's like if we inundated you with music that was more than your eardrums could handle, your eardrum would rupture. Your physical makeup couldn't tolerate that. This is a silly example, but the vibration, the consciousness, has to be aligned with the ability to be relocated to this other actual place that exists in a higher frequency. Does that make sense, is that clear?

J: Yes, thank you. We do understand the limitations of the translation of what you see from your perspective and dimension, Subconscious, to you know, us little monkey minds. So I understand.

A: Well it's not that, there are some limitations, so thank you for recognizing.

J: Well, I respect that, and I respect all the information you give to us because it's very helpful for us to be prepared for this relocation. Subconscious, can you advise me about the life contract for the soul of this planet in terms of relocating to the fifth dimension? Can you give me a summary of what's going on there?

A: Do we understand that you're asking about the physical planet of Earth, it's soul Gaia, about her soul contract?

J: Yes and how does, within her soul contract, her moving to a fifth dimension or relocating, can you help us understand this?

A: That's, even for us, that's really big. That's really complex because the soul of a planet is choosing when it's time for a relocation, so to speak. Reincarnation, or you know, moving to the next life form vessel, that soul leaving is something big. It's big enough for you guys, but for us, you know it's quite a phenomenal situation. It's not something common at all. We're just reaching out to the collectives, all the collective consciousness to see what information... It's a spectacular event because the Earth and incarnation of Gaia and Earth is so beautiful, and it's been more than a millennium. But Earth is, this is not accurate, but if God had a favorite, a favorite kid — there's something so special and beautiful and unique and different about Earth. It's numerous, innumerable, the Galaxy is unfathomable, even at our higher level of understanding, it's still so — there's so much awe. But that little tiny third rock from the sun, so to speak, has such enormous, there's so much power and beauty and Source energy that is inherent to humanity and so many other galactic or celestial beings. But there's... I'm not finding the words, or the right way again, forgive me.

J: I think you're doing a really great job, Subconscious. It truly is a beyond awesome experience.

A: It is so big for us, even ourselves, we're in awe of it, so it's hard to adequately explain because this doesn't happen galactically. This is not, this is new, and you know for the Universe to be something as very old as timeless, for something NEW—is strange for us. Does that make sense? For something new to occur that we've...that's never been witnessed—is peculiar and intriguing and curious and fascinating to us as well.

J: Is it because the soul is shifting into a higher dimension with this reincarnation?

A: The soul of a planet is consciously deciding to leave the vessel for a new higher frequency. Yes, yes, this is the easy answer to your question. But it's typically, with planets, the soul of the planet, if it has one, the soul will just like, I mean... the thoughts, the answer is there, it's just she's having a hard time organizing them into cohesive—so just to just allow us a moment...

We'll go back to the simple answers, yes, it's because she is elevating. Her transition is to a higher consciousness instead of a lateral move out of a dying body. The other planet is dying, that planet's soul, typically that's not an upgrade, it's a lateral move. Does that even equate to anything that makes any sense at all?

J: It does, thank you, thank you very much. I do appreciate that, and so, Subconscious, we use the term "Old Earth", and we would like to understand, from your perspective, what is that referring to?

A: The term you use, the Old Earth, is the current one, where you all reside. You say old, I mean I guess it is old, but y'all say that in comparison to what you foresee is New Earth. I guess when Gaia is complete, when there's no more life and humanity no longer exists on this particular planetary galactic formation. So you call it Old

Earth because you know you're receiving that there's a new one. So what else would you call it, current Earth—it's where you are, it's where you all are currently residing in your 3D, in their 3D life.

J: Will there be an event that will take place that would sort of occur to us to then start labeling this planet the Old Earth experience?

A: Well you're already calling it Old Earth, but obviously once everyone has been relocated to what is referred to as New Earth this would indeed be the Old Earth. But this, in the way that you know it, in the way that you recognize or feel like you know it, what you've experienced of this 3D planet with your 3D existence, your experience—this would no longer exist in the way that you know it.

J: Okay, when people, instead of reincarnating, people have been preparing to shift, and have been shifting for quite some years. Is that what you would perceive as an accurate statement?

A: Yes, the process is in progress. There was a point for you all where the reincarnation cycle stopped, and so those whose souls have left, and then they've chosen yes to the 5D Earth. There are souls that have transitioned there, as much of Gaia is inhabiting this, her new vessel.

J: Thank you so much, I understand. Okay, so then you're saying to us that the New Earth is a completely different existence than the Old Earth or the current Earth we're living in now?

A: Yes.

the SHIFT to NEW EARTH

J: So it's a new planet?

A: Yes, yes, it's like a new baby, and life is free. The soul was given to that new vessel. It's a place that is not here. It is a place, a physical one, and that's kind of a 3D term, but it is a location that is not where you are right now. Where this is, it is not in the same location of the... again I'm going to hate to use this term, but the third rock from the sun. It is not in the same location as the Earth as you all have known it to be—it's in a very different location.

J: Thank you, okay, so can you give me some examples of the differences in the way of living on the New Earth from how we live on this current Earth?

A: There's such a vast difference between 3D and the higher you go, dimensions and elevations. Hard to conceptualize, but simply, it's a place where humans, mankind as we call it, will exist within the nature that Source intended for humanity, without interference from any other motivations. Where there is true connection to one another through the Source, which is love. It will be more harmonious. It will even look visually different, how do we say for you guys to understand through your 3D eyes—it'll be sparklier, it'll be brighter, it'll be colors that you've never imagined, that you can't imagine with where you are, and that's okay. Lighter, and I mean your physical form and the atmosphere. You'll better understand unconditional love and acceptance of one another. It's truly just what Source created humanity for, or what we believe you guys were meant to be. Much like there are a lot of other collectives that are truly just benevolence and love for one another. There will be a better understanding, communication with Gaia or with the soul, with your home. You'll be in better communication with, we'll just say Earth, and all of its inhabitants. Any of the flora and the fauna that exist there, because you'll still enjoy plants and trees and wildlife and vegetation and animals. There may be some you've never seen before, they may look different, but there will be such a harmony and in communication and just a heart centered connection to your surroundings. Every living entity, everything is alive, as it is here, but you'll understand more. There will be just a natural knowing, and that's such a peaceful joyous revelation of understanding. It's like an aha moment— like "This is who we were created to be and how we were created". So there's so much more joy and genuine love and peacefulness and again the word communal comes to mind. Communal living in communities, taking care of one another. With your elevated, improved bodies, there won't be the sickness or the failure that happens to these biological bodies you currently reside, your current vessels, there won't be the breakdowns— because you'll have evolved spiritually, to a different level. You won't carry things that cause harm to your body. You'll be more in tune with the vessel that carries your essence. You'll be more one.

J: Thank you, can you tell me more about that vessel that we will be carrying on the New Earth?

A: Crystalline, crystalline not carbon-based.

J: Can you give the vehicle a sense of being there now, and can she be able to express, through you, what her first noticing experiences are being on the New Earth?

A: She sees just like a prism of light. Everyone is not the same, but everyone is so similar. These crystalline bodies are so effervescent and beautiful. But just like here, no soul is the same, so the vessel that harbors it will also not be exactly alike. You'll be able to differentiate. You'll know one another based on more of a soul level. But, I'm sorry, I'm straying from your question. She's saying that there's no hair on a crystalline body. They're just brimming with vitality and health, and there's a shimmer. Not transparent, but it's as if— you take a prism in every fractal of color that you shine light on it. They're just more like light beings with form and she's seeing them as just some beautifully colored— she wants to say tie-dyed, but it's colorful. It's crisp and clear. There's a uniformity, but we don't want to imply that everyone is a, haha no pun intended, "carbon copy", and it's not like everyone looks exactly the same. We're struggling, she's struggling... sorry.

J: I understand, it is a big concept to try and translate, when it is so different. and from this perspective so foreign to our normal way of describing physical bodies. Can you give her a sneak peek of the New Earth, and can she be able to tell through you— how does she feel when she is looking at this new planet?

A: There aren't adequate words because the beauty is so indescribable. There's no way to adequately express it, that you can even understand that at all. She's just feeling filled with this sense of love and awe and beauty that's just beyond anything we can even grapple with, because it's so... Source. Source is so palpable and evident. In communication with Gaia when we get to experience and be so much more a part, physically close to that Source of love and all that is. The essence is overwhelming and so beautiful.

J: Wonderful, thank you so much. Out of curiosity, would we be able to take our current bodies to the New Earth?

A: These bodies are not capable of withstanding the, I'll use your word "shift", they couldn't, they would break down. They would not be able to exist in that vibration. Again, what we said earlier, like if we turned up music so loud that your eardrums would rupture, your eardrums couldn't handle such a high frequency or vibration. It's the same, just amplified. You know, exponentially, these bodies that you live in right now are suited for this— the 3D where you live, and sometimes not even that well. But no, these physical bodies where you are now would not tolerate the higher vibrational frequency of the 5D. They're not composed of the proper, what makes up this body that you live in. It would not be compatible with that of a different higher frequency.

J: Okay, thank you. Subconscious, we hear from many other people who are talking about the New Earth, they're saying that the New Earth here is on this planet now and that we are in the fifth dimension. Where are they getting their information from?

A: There are a lot of well-intended, highly spiritual folks that we can't say with any degree of certainty overall, where they're getting their particular information from. I think there are a lot of souls with the best of intentions, and they're trying to raise their vibration which is appropriate. But they're misled in thinking by living in a higher state of vibration that they're already experiencing (5D). They may be healthier in their physical body and spiritually and emotionally — in all the ways, you know, they may be a healthier essence because they're paying attention, feeding this body better, feeding their spirit, you know, so they may feel a bit more enlightened, or even lighter, so they mistakenly mislabel that as "I'm advancing, so this must be 5D. I'm in a state of love, I've done my inner work. There's peace and love within me, so that must be. I'm seeing people differently. I'm loving people differently and that must be what 5D Earth looks like, and so it's here". That's our best understanding that we can give her to express. She's thinking, she's interrupting here. She's thinking, wondering if you're thinking of anybody in particular that thinks they're involved. Send her back, get her out of here!

J: Okay, well, she can relax and enjoy the way it feels to have no problems and no worries and nothing to think about as we have the conversation with her Subconscious today. So thank you, Subconscious, for all of that. That is really helpful to be able to get another perspective and another set of descriptions for what we keep hearing in many sessions from other Subconsciouses, so thank you. Is there a message that you would like to share for humanity today?

A: We're here, we're here as we always have been. You all have so much love directed, like love bombed at you all. So seek us out, pray, meditate, work on letting go of your crap. That's what holds you, that is actual gravity, and that holds you down in every sense of the word. So continue to seek out your inner peace, your highest power, your higher consciousness, continue to ask questions, continue to let go of that which no longer serves you. In the end there is an overall growth spike. There is a vibration that's increasing, it's elevating and it's exciting. And so many of you feel that there's something happening at large, not every soul is there—

the SHIFT to NEW EARTH

but be patient with one another. Love one another unconditionally without judgment, without any barriers. Continue to love each other, uplift each other, educate each other, inform, enlighten, support, but don't judge and just give yourself a break— it's not a race. This is not a race. It will all happen as it is supposed to. Be at peace with yourself, knowing that you are loved beyond measure and enjoy, enjoy the ride, enjoy the show.

J: Thank you so much, I really appreciate all the information you have provided for us today.

Session 9

J: I'd like to call upon the Subconscious.

C: Yes.

J: Thank you. Are you able to do a body scan for the vehicle, please, and be able to tell me everything that's going on for the vehicle?

C: She is very relaxed.

J: Wonderful, is there anything that needs to be healed or balanced?

C: Yes, her shoulder bothers her a lot, but we've let her know that we're going to continue leaving it the way it is.

J: Is it possible for you to be able to lessen the intensity of that discomfort for her?

C: Yes, we can do that.

J: Fantastic. She is very much aware and always will be aware that she is in the third dimension, so are you able to just support her a little bit more with comfort of the body and any other aspects that she is having with the body?

C: Yes, we can do that.

J: Wonderful, is there anything else you'd like me to know about the body?

C: She is feeling the dizziness.

J: Tell me why she is getting the sense of dizziness.

C: We get that she's connecting in, and it's throwing her a little bit off balance.

J: Connecting into what? That is making her out of balance?

C: Connecting into other people's energies. She does need to ground.

J: More is it because she hasn't? It's just starting to come spring for her, so she hasn't been able to do her normal routine of grounding?

C: She hasn't been spending as much time grounding as she needs to. She does absorb a lot of energy when she goes out because she makes a special effort to get in touch with people and make eye contact, and she absorbs a lot of their stuff.

J: She's definitely amazing. If she can't keep going outside, on a rainy day, for example, how else can she ground when she can't get outside?

C: We've told her before she can ground through us. She just needs to ask. She just needs to ask, and even when it's raining, she can go outside. It's a choice.

J: Thank you, we understand, and she will be grateful for this reminder. Thank you so much. We know that it is significant and purposeful for her to be reminded of this today. So with this dizziness, can you help us understand, is this necessary for her to feel this, because it does seem like it gives her some discomfort as well in some regards?

C: If she grounds more, it won't be as severe. We'll work on it with her.

J: Wonderful, is there anything else that's happening to her body that you would like to balance and heal?

C: She knows that she needs to work on not eating as much sugar.

J: What is the need for her to have that little amount of sugar she does consume?

C: A lot of it is a habit, sometimes it's a craving.

J: Is this a problem for her body, Subconscious, or would you like it to be resolved today?

C: No, she's doing okay. She can cut back, but she's doing okay. There's times that she'd binge. She doesn't feel good after, so she knows not to do that.

J: Okay, well, that's great that she is so in tune with her body that she knows the difference between 'good' and 'bad'. She does deserve treats as well, so what would you recommend if she was trying to have a little treat?

C: She tried apples, but whatever's on the apples was giving her cankers in her mouth. So now she's on to tapioca pudding. As long as she does it in moderation, she's okay.

J: Brilliant, well, thank you for the great news. Are we able to start asking the questions for the session, or was there something else you'd like to heal and balance in her body now?

C: We'll work on her as you go, go ahead.

J: Brilliant, thank you so much. Subconscious, I really appreciate that. Subconscious, can you let me know what dimension you are in?

C: Seventh.

J: Thank you so much, and Subconscious, from your perspective in terms of the "shift", what does shifting to 5D mean for humanity?

C: Releasing the density. Releasing the bodies that they have now. Going to a lighter body. Learning how to experience without all the density that they've been going through all this time. A new school.

J: Thank you so much. Are you able to advise me, and tell me what the life contract for this planet's soul is, in terms of shifting to 5D, so we can understand what is Gaia's life contract to shift to 5D?

C: She has already shifted, not much is left here. Her life contract changed when this planet became so dense and so damaged. She's finally, finally at peace. She's getting ready for humanity to come to those that chose it.

J: Thank you, and in terms of the 'Old Earth', what is that referring to, the 'Old Earth'?

C: Learning experiences for the people who are contracted to stay behind, who have chosen to stay behind to learn more, to experience more. Some of them have chosen to stay to assist the people that are still learning and to learn more of their own experiences.

J: Thank you, could you give me some examples of what lessons and experiences people want to experience on the Old Earth?

C: There will be a lot of awakening, a lot of realizing. The things that they have been taught all this time have been untrue. They will be finishing their life contracts learning how to release and let go so that they can shift also.

J: Fantastic, thank you. Is there anything else people will be learning on the Old Earth?

C: I feel there will be a lot more bonding with people, with each other a lot. More of getting together and communicating instead of judging. Finding peace. Finding community.

J: I love that. Okay, that's fantastic. Thank you, would there be an event that takes place that would officially make us start calling the Earth experience Old Earth?

C: We're hearing the laser event and the trumpet, or as you refer to it, the speaker[18]. Once a lot of people have shifted from that event, then it will be the official Old Earth.

J: Thank you, is there anything you can tell me about the trumpet?

---

[18] A noise which is heard around the world— is from another session where this large group of people shift, where people can hear this event around the world. Turning the atmosphere into a speaker.

C: Not everyone will hear it. Those who will hear it will know it's time to ascend, to shift, to move on to their next part of their journeys

J: Thank you, do you get a sense of what is making the sound of the trumpet?

C: It is coming out from an island somewhere. Out in the ocean, a sound will come from there. We're not sure exactly where or when.

J: Will the vehicle hear the sound of this trumpet?

C: Some will. Those who are meant to hear it will hear it.

J: What's the significance of those who get to hear it?

C: They will know it's time.

J: I see. Fascinating, thank you so much, and so, Subconscious, what is New Earth?

C: A new learning, a higher dimension, 5D learning and relearning, experiencing, experimentation with new things. A new stepping stone on the journey can be an incredible experience, and it will be for all those who are meant to go there. For all those who have life contracts to go up to 5D.

J: Thank you, how would you describe the New Earth?

C: Beautiful, lush brilliant colors. High energy. Loving, very loving. An incredible place to go and learn and to experience high energy.

J: Thank you, it sounds amazing. Are there any differences between the way we're living on this Earth now versus New Earth?

C: Yes. There will be telepathy. We will learn how to create things with our minds and we will learn how to communicate without speaking. We won't need to eat like we do on planet Earth. The energy level will be so much higher, and it won't be dense, and it won't be damaging. Incredible energy, high vibrational beauty. All those who go there will have an incredible experience.

J: Thank you so much. Subconscious, are you able to give the vehicle a peek at the New Earth please?

C: She doesn't do visuals, but she's been seeing some visuals in her mind as we've been speaking of it.

J: Wonderful, what is she noticing?

C: She's noticing that the garden she spoke of in her book is there. It's been recreated there. The brilliant colors, the fairies. She's seeing all kinds of incredible things there not visually, just in her mind.

J: I understand. How does she feel, then, sensing around on New Earth?

C: Peace and love, peace and love.

J: Beautiful. In her garden, it was from her other lifetime that she's now recreated on the New Earth? Is that what you want me to understand?

C: She was given memories of lives that other people lived, that other people experienced at higher dimensions. That's what she wrote about in her book. She could visualize it as she wrote it. She didn't actually live that life experience, but she experienced it through someone else.

J: I see, did we explore that in another session where she was a fairy in Ireland, when she had the fairy imprint life?

C: Her fairy life was a walk-in and a walkout.

J: I understand. Okay, well, thank you, and so has she been able to recreate that garden from those lifetimes?

C: Yes, and her imagination, and in one of the books that Sylvia Brown wrote about. When she was talking with her spirit guide, she was describing a garden like that, too, so she pulled from that also.

J: Wonderful.

C: And the fairies were added in because of her love of that part lifetime experience.

J: And remind me, again, of her love and her true connection to the fairies? Can you remind me of the significance of that?

C: Her fairy life was a journey she took for relaxation, and so that she could view humans from a different perspective, plus she needed the community of the fairies and the peace. It was almost like a vacation for her.

J: Wonderful, okay, how marvelous to be able to recreate the garden. Yes. Is there anything else you'd like to know about what she does on the New Earth?

C: She won't be there for very long. She wanted to experience being there because of all the times she's been supporting humanity on this planet. She wanted to be there to greet them.

J: Beautiful, is there anything else you'd like to remind her about, what she does after New Earth?

C: I think she takes a little bit of time there, but not long. She's ready to move on to the next thing.

the SHIFT to NEW EARTH

J: Are we able to know what the next thing could be for her?

C: Yes, she will be guiding and doing the things that she did for planet Earth somewhere else. It's her purpose and her love.

J: Fantastic, thank you so much. I really appreciate that. So out of curiosity, Subconscious, will we be able to take our current bodies on to New Earth?

C: No, these bodies are too dense for that high vibration. We don't see that happening. The New Earth energy vibrations would be too high for a carbon-based 3D body to be there.

J: The bodies we will be having on the New Earth, what can you tell me about them?

C: Higher vibrational, not as dense. They will be crystalline bodies.

J: Subconscious, we hear many other people talking about New Earth being here now on this planet and that we are in the fifth dimension. Where are they getting the information from?

C: We're hearing the word hopium. We think that they just aren't open to the fact that Earth is way too dense to ever repair in this lifetime. They're hoping, because they're so attached to their lives that they can stay here. A lot of the people that are saying they're in 5D are doing it for the money. Doing it for the followers. Even if they raise their vibrations, they're still living in a 3D body, and you can't be in 5D with a 3D body, in a 3D experience on a 3D Earth.

J: Would you be able to explain to us what a 5D mindset is here on this current planet?

C: She just thought she felt in 5D at times, and she's right. When her vibrations are raised, and when she's feeling really, really good, she could feel that she was in 5D— if she believed what everyone was saying. But she knows she's still living this 3D experience, so she has the understanding that that's what they're feeling. They're feeling the high vibrations, and they're feeling like they're there, and they've achieved it, and they're awake. But they're still living in a 3D body on a 3D planet— so they're not in 5D.

J: When she is in the mindset of a fifth dimensional realm, what's the percentage of her days or time that she is able to maintain that?

C: Not long, because then she goes back out into the world, or she goes out into the other room where her husband or her mother are, and she comes back down, because they're very stuck in 3D, and that's okay. That's their experience, and it's meant to be that way for her, too.

J: She's so wonderful. She needed to be able to help us, as people in the 3D, that's for sure in my opinion.

C: She just had a moment where she was saying 'no pedestals'.

J: Subconscious, could it be said that she is a pretty special gift to humanity?

C: She is, and she understands that, but she also lives in the 3D, so she has her doubts, and that's okay.

J: Could we help release some of those doubts please? I think that would help her greatly?

C: Yes, they don't happen very often. It's usually when she has a confrontation with her mom or her husband that she feels like she's got a lot of work to do.

J: Okay, well, thank you very much. Subconscious, is there anything you would like us to learn or know about today?

C: We tell her all the time everything is under control. Her statement that she has written on her desk is "All is Well," and the statement that you continue to say: all is really well. You just have to have patience, and sometimes that's not easy, but when it's meant to happen, it will happen.

J: Is there anything we can do to be able to help get to that point of getting it happening?

C: She can continue doing what she's doing and just love, just love, spread the love wherever she goes. As far as you keep having things come up for you to where you know what you're meant to ask, and your teams are showing you what you're meant to ask and who you're meant to bring in. A lot of things have to fall into place before the shift, and you both know that.

J: For all those fantastic experiences, because it's all purposeful.

C: Yes, it is.

J: We're not complaining, we promise. Subconscious, we appreciate all of the life experiences we get, and we are very much looking forward to seeing how it all unfolds.

C: Some complaining is okay, that's 3D.

J: Well, thank you! We appreciate that, we'll take that! Okay, well, thank you so much.

Session 10

J: I'd like to call upon the Subconscious, please.

K: Yes.

J: Thank you. Are you able to please do a body scan for the vehicle, and tell me what is happening for her?

K: There's lots of toxins in her body. She needs to clear out her body by eating a lot better than what she has been. She's been emotionally eating, and it's crippling her.

J: Why has she been emotionally eating?

K: Her depression is creeping back a little bit. But it's gonna be okay.

J: What is causing the depression?

K: She feels like she's incapable of succeeding with this spirituality. She feels like she's not progressing as well as she should be, but there is no target to meet. She can just pace herself. There's no expectations. She's creating the expectations in her mind.

J: So, in reality, Subconscious, from your perspective, how is her spirituality journey going?

K: It's progressing as quickly and as slowly as it's supposed to be. It takes time, but she feels like she has to rush, and it's overwhelming her because she wants to do it faster.

J: Why does she feel like she needs to do it faster?

K: She wants to be able to find her ability and be able to use it, but she can't hurry that long. So just pace, just pace, and things will happen for her as they are meant to. They won't happen any sooner than they're meant to. It's not something you can rush. Just do a little bit each day.

J: Subconscious do you think that her worrying about this is actually limiting her, versus if she sort of stopped having this judgment on self— she could expand easier?

K: She needs to stop worrying about not doing it fast enough. She feels like she's not awakened, but she is. It goes back to that belief in self. She does love herself more and that's where the most important thing begins— is with self-love. We are very happy that it's improved. But she also needs to stop worrying, just relax.

J: Now that she hears that and understands that, can you advise me of whether that depression she was feeling will be lifted and released now?

K: We will guide her. We're showing her a window, and we're opening up the window, and we want the worries and concerns to blow out the window. They are not for holding, there's no justification for holding onto them. We want her to release, and we're just releasing that now.

J: Beautiful, thank you so much, Subconscious. Is there anything else that's happening in her body that you can assist her to have today as we are seeking balance and harmony?

K: The food intake needs to improve, and it will now that we have started to release the worries, because that saying "you are what you eat," well, she's eating comfort

the SHIFT to NEW EARTH

food, which is creating toxins in her body, was putting toxins in her body, which is creating a... it's like creating a negative aura around her body, and that's where her hip pain is really centered. So every time or every day that it gets worse, the pain gets worse, it's just her body. It's telling her to clean up her diet. The meat that she's eating, and she's eating the meat because her Dad has purchased a lot of really good quality meat where he works. She feels like she has to eat it because it's there, and it was a gift from her Dad, but she can't. Her body actually can't take that anymore, because spiritually she's above and beyond the need of red meat, any meat really. So she needs to stop eating that which is causing her— it's causing her pain, but spiritually wise, it's creating a block between her, her mind and us. When I say us, I say her Subconscious, her higher self, and the communication between her mind and her guides. It's like when you cook something fatty, and you get that grease that's left over in the pan, that grease is the blockage. It's creating a blockage. So we just want her to stop eating the meat and the chocolate and anything else that she thinks is making her feel better. Because we're trying to get through to her, and we can't when those blocks are in place. Drink more water.

J: How much water does she need to drink per day?

K: It's a minimum of two liters, but we really want her to drink more. She's feeding the water to her plants, but she needs it for her body as well. We want her to get a really big drink bottle so she can monitor herself. That's the best way, otherwise she doesn't know how many glasses she's drinking throughout the day because there's no accountability. Accountability isn't a bad thing, it's just a way for her to make sure that she's giving her body what she needs.

J: Thank you so much, okay, is there anything else you'd like us to know about her body?

K: We want her to visualize daily just her body lifting off the ground and just floating through the air because that will help her to lift those worries and concerns.

J: I love that, thank you so much, Subconscious. Are we able to continue on and ask the questions for this session?

K: Yes, we would like to work on her hip.

J: Yes, please, are you able to work on her body completely, releasing all that no longer serves her, and balance her completely and all of her physical systems and energetic systems as you see fit?

K: Thank you, yes.

J: Thank you, okay. Subconscious, out of curiosity, what dimension are you in?

K: We are in the sixth.

J: Thank you so much, and from your perspective, Subconscious, in terms of the "shift", what does shifting to 5D mean for humanity?

K: It's like it's a snake shedding its skin, or a caterpillar turning into a butterfly. When we shift, we leave the shell, and we move out of that shell. We transcend into a higher and better version of ourselves. Imagine your body is laying still on the bed. As the shift occurs, the

the SHIFT to NEW EARTH

body stays there, but our soul lifts and continues living—but in a better, higher, more stable and loving version of the Earth that we know now. Does that answer your question?

J: Yes, is there anything else you'd like us to know about the shift for humanity?

K: Humanity needs to realize what they're living now, it is such a trap. There are forces that are trying to keep the masses down in the 3D consciousness to keep themselves wealthy and powerful and in charge. They are afraid of losing that power because they are so used to it. It's all they know. But humanity needs to move away from that. It can't last forever, but it needs to happen sooner rather than later. Because the planet's soul is shifting, it's peeling away, it's peeling away the negativity and we want everyone to, or as many people, to lift with the New Earth. Which at the moment looks like a hologram, the way we're sort of showing her, it's like a hologram peeling away. It's like a magnet, it's trying to bring as many people as possible with it. Does that answer your question?

J: Yes, I know these are broad questions, so thank you. And then can you tell me about Gaia's contract to shift to the fifth dimension? What would you like us to understand about that?

K: So we're just showing her Gaia as a female energy, and she's hovering away from us, facing us, but she's holding on to this hologram that we mentioned before. Helping it peel away from this Earth, and she's just getting ready to place herself within the New Earth. But she is watching, she's watching from the outside, but attached to both, barely. It's like her fingertips are just touching both, and she's transitioning out of one and getting ready to go into the other. But it's just her fingertips. We all want as many people as possible to join the New Earth, and it's happening, it's slowly happening. There's more and more people awakening, but the word 'trigger', we're just showing her the word 'trigger'. There needs to be a trigger, because we just need more people to awaken.

J: And when more people awaken, what will happen then?

K: The Old Earth will be left to its own devices. Would you like us to see what's actually happening around the Earth as the shift progresses, is that what you want us to see and tell you about?

J: You're very clever because the very next question is about what is the term 'Old Earth' referring to?

K: The Old Earth will be like dusty old furniture. Still there, but it will be quite useless. It won't be completely unusable, but it would be useless for the future. We don't see much happening on the Old Earth, once we all shift our consciousness and our bodies into the New Earth. The New Earth will be vibrant and quite energized, but the Old Earth will be rendered useless. There will be parts of it that you can see, lava, and I guess I can see like lava cooling, cooling off. And then the majority of the Earth is just dusty, unusable, livable but not vibrant, not healthy, and it won't last for long. Whereas the New Earth, as it peels away, it distances itself from the Old Earth. If I put myself on the New Earth, I can slowly see the Old Earth just moving away slowly. But if we put ourselves back onto the Old Earth, we can see the New Earth again moving away, but it's very energetic. It's buzzing, I think is the word we'll use. It's buzzing with energy. So indeed, the Old Earth is very dense, very dark like it looks like it's just throwing out shadow. There's no light, there's no life. The planet itself is very lifeless. Does that answer your question?

J: Thank you, would there be an event to take place that would then create us to label this planet 'Old Earth'?

K: There will be many, there will be many. There won't be one big event, it'll be one event that causes a domino effect. But it will feel, I guess it will feel like one event. But it will actually be many that will create that domino effect. I can see dominoes falling around the globe.

J: Thank you. Could you give us from your perspective, please, Subconscious, some of the life lessons people would experience on the Old Earth?

K: We would like everyone to learn to forgive. Because a lot of the contracts have to do with past lives and things that have happened in past lives. We see a lot of people stuck or trapped on this Earth who need to forgive those who have done the wrong thing to them. We will use examples, so if let's say in this lifetime, your mother who was a brother in the past lifetime, had murdered you in the past lifetime, and you have both come back in this lifetime to learn about forgiveness, learn about love and learn to live with each other in a loving, peaceful way. Then that is what you need to learn, love and forgiveness. And a lot of people are refusing to move on with love and with forgiveness, and they're holding on to that hate, that negativity, and they're refusing to release it. We really, really need people to step into the light, and the light resembles the love, and the future. We want people to turn their backs on the past and when they turn their back on the past, it means that they are willing to move forward and step into the light, and hold hands with the person that is, you know, is causing the pain or had caused the pain. Hold their hand and help them step into the light. Because they're also struggling to see that the past is in the past, and the future just holds so much more than that hate and the negativity that they are holding on to. It will help others see that they can do it too. If we can do it, they can do it. And if we take the first step, then the other person might take the next step, and then the future steps can be taken together. Does that make sense?

J: Thank you, it does. I mean it's all great information and perspectives to be able to consider and understand and put into place, so thank you, thank you very much. Is there anything else you'd like us to know about the Old Earth?

K: The Old Earth has so much healing to do, and it's not going to heal whilst we're still on here.

J: Okay, thank you. Subconscious, can you tell me what New Earth is?

K: It is a spiritual being that encompasses our abilities. It is love. It is like heaven, if you could imagine heaven, what heaven means for us as individuals and as a collective, and what we were raised to believe heaven is — that's the New Earth.

J: Okay, what else can you tell me about the New Earth? How would you describe it?

K: It is not a solid thing like the Old Earth.

J: Okay, in terms of the location between the New Earth and the Old Earth, what can you tell me about that?

K: It's like we mentioned before, it's peeling away from the Old Earth. It's in another dimension, but Gaia is holding onto both. Does that make sense?

J: In terms of what we would perceive as the universe, is it very vast from your perspective, in terms of different locations, or how can you help me understand?

K: Are you asking if it's physically in a different location? Physically it's right here, because it's still detaching itself.

J: Are you talking about the soul of the planet, or?

K: Yes, physically as in its solid form. It is not in our solar system.

J: The New Earth?

K: The new one.

J: So I know we can't really understand or conceive time and space, but am I to understand that the New Earth is not physically here on this Earth?

K: No, it's removing itself, it's completely removing itself. This planet has been destroyed to the point where it's not usable and it can only be healed if it's left alone over many millions of years. And so the New Earth has to shift into something completely different and go to somewhere completely different. The way to get there is through spirituality, hence the spiritual detachment of Old Earth and New Earth, and our bodies and our spiritual bodies.

J: And so how do people shift? How can you help us understand that?

K: It's like the snake skin. Our bodies will be left here, and our consciousness will shift to the New Earth. So we're just seeing bodies left behind. The physical bodies, they're just, they're just the outer layer, and our consciousness, our souls, rising away from the Earth constantly. Like a constant, as a continuation of people in their spiritual form, leaving the Earth, and they're going into the light, which takes them to the New Earth if they wish to. So it's like a portal, the light is like a portal to the New Earth, if that makes sense?

J: And where is this portal?

K: It's in the sky. It's about the same distance from the Earth as the moon.

J: And will people see it or sense it?

K: They will be drawn to it, it's like a magnet. But there are some people that are kind of... just before they get to the light they peel away and they go to other places.

J: Thank you so much. You've just said that we will leave our current bodies behind, and from my understanding we would call the current bodies we're in carbon-based bodies. So the new bodies we get, what can you tell me about that?

K: They will be, I guess we can compare it to a ghost. It will be in that form, where we are physically here on the Old Earth able to leave, but we don't have a physical body such as the one that we have now. Because we won't need it.

J: Can you tell me more about the new bodies and what they would appear like or how would they feel?

K: You can see them glowing, but they are a little bit translucent as well. But it's only for a period of time because there is a transition at some point. It's a transition depending on what level of consciousness we're at. And it depends on what choices we make. So we can choose to have the bodies that we had when we left or our original. Depending on where we came from. Does that make sense?

J: Yes, it sounds very valid. We're very curious to know what certain bodies will look like, but I guess it's one of those things that we have to wait and see.

K: It will not be like anything that you have experienced here on this Earth.

J: Okay, thank you, and out of curiosity, can someone take a carbon-based body to the New Earth?

K: No, we can't travel through space with these bodies physically.

J: Okay, thank you, are you able please to give the vehicle a sense of being on the New Earth now and are you able to tell us what she is sensing as she is arriving on the New Earth?

K: Okay, just give us a minute. It feels very weird, her body is actually, the sensation she's got right now is that she's being spun around really fast, and she's dizzy. Just give us a minute, sorry.

J: Okay, well, we don't want to make you feel ill. Subconscious, are you able to just give her the senses of the feeling of New Earth? What it will feel like for her to arrive on the New Earth?

K: It will feel empty at first. It's hard to say, it's hard to say at the moment, but she will feel like she's got work to do. We are involved in helping people to transition onto the New Earth, so for her in particular, it'll feel in a good way, like she's going to work. But like we said, it's in a good way, it's pleasurable.

J: Okay, and what are her senses with the feelings of that fifth dimension?

K: Positive, good. Ambitious and happy that finally we can start the process of bringing people on by the masses. Because there's people already there when she arrives, but it's not the masses you know. So to answer your question, it feels rather empty and dark because it's hidden at the time. But once the masses start arriving, everything will be bright and beautiful as she has seen it before.

J: Okay, thank you. So if you could give her a sense of later, within the experience of the New Earth, what will she notice when it's more established?

K: It'll be busy, but it'll be so much different to the Old Earth. So to try and explain, we'll do it by comparing the happiness and the joy. Imagine you are on holidays with your family. Let's say you're at the beach, and you're relaxing, and your kids are around you, and everyone's happy just enjoying yourselves, and the smell in the air is fresh and clean — that is kind of what it's going to be like for everyone on the New Earth. There's no rush, there's no sense of, you know, if someone steps in front of you and you get frustrated — there's none of that. It's just everyone living with each other and putting up with each other in a positive way. There's no negativity. Does that answer your question?

J: Thank you so much, and out of curiosity, Subconscious, there's many people talking about the New Earth being here and that they're already on the New Earth and that they are in the fifth dimension. Where are they getting this information from?

K: It's a misunderstanding, it's a misguided misunderstanding. To get to the New Earth, the physical body has to so-called die and our spiritual bodies move on. They continue living, it's a continuation. There is no death in the spiritual body. But for our spiritual bodies to be able to get to the New Earth, we physically need to awaken our soul. So we need to have an understanding here now that...we're sorry, we're trying to find the words... It needs to be an awakening on this Earth. Each individual needs to awaken to the knowing and understanding of what happens to us when our body dies. We need to also prepare our 5D bodies for the transition. So that's where we need to understand that we need to get away from the negativity, the politics, the black versus whites, the food that we put into our bodies, they are designed to keep us feeling low —that's depression, that's anxiety. We need to move away from that and connect with ourselves spiritually. So meditation, raw fresh food, you know, heal our past lives — so if you have karma attached to you, that's the example we used earlier, where if you were killed by say your sister in the past life and that sister in your past life is now your mother — you need to heal that relationship.

That will help the transitioning of the 3D into the 5D. And the more of that we can heal and live by now, the faster you will be able to move into the 5D. Does that answer your question?

J: Thank you, so the events that occur, do they not help us shift to the 5D? We must do it individually?

K: They can help if you are ready at the time of the event. Essentially we are all preparing for the event. Our event. My event is not necessarily someone else's event. So when my event happens and I have spiritually prepared myself for it — yes, I can go to the 5D. If I haven't prepared myself, then I will go into what we call a ship. It is the in-between, and I can complete that transition and go to the 5D from there. There are people who will refuse to. This is very complicated. There are some people who will refuse to shift, and will also refuse to go to the ship to help them transition to the 5D Earth. Those people will stay on the 3D as long as they refuse to budge, if that makes sense? There is so much more to it that we lack the vocabulary to explain. But in a nutshell, that's the rule of thumb. If you haven't spiritually prepared yourself, there is the option of either staying, or going to the ships where you can continue the transition. But if you have prepared yourself, if you are awakened, and when we say awakened, we mean the understanding that you are ready, willing and want to go to the 5D, you can go there. It's like religion when people believe in heaven and hell and all that in-between. If they believe that when they die they go to heaven, that is kind of them ready for death, and willing to die, and happy to die in their physical form, because they know that they are going somewhere that they want to go. So when you have people here on Earth who say no, there is no such thing as 5D, there is no such thing as heaven, there is no such thing as a transition to the 5D, well, they are leaving themselves attached to the 3D, to the lower vibration, and therefore they are stuck. But the event that will happen to that person, and it will happen, it's inevitable, in that moment in time, they will have to make the choice of either staying in their non-physical form here on the 3D until they are ready to move on, or they can go onto the ship. Most people will, who are in that sort of situation, where they have to make a choice of "what do you want to do, are you ready yet or do you want to stay here?" The majority will go to the ships. But more and more people are awakening, and therefore, they won't need to make that choice. They will just naturally be magnetized to the light that we showed her before, and that we described to you before. Does that make sense?

J: Indeed. It's all very fascinating. Thank you so much.

K: It is extremely complicated. It's such a different thing from anything that you can imagine, and the descriptive words that we have here in front of us to use do not come close to describing what it is that is actually going to take place. We can't tell you exactly when everything is going to happen and how it's going to happen. We can only give you the idea of — it will happen soon, and it will kind of look like this. Does that make sense?

J: Thank you, in terms of you stating it will happen soon, what sort of reference point is soon?

K: There are many things happening right now on Earth that we cannot reveal to the vessel or potentially anyone's ears that may come across this recording. So we will say that there are things happening right now that need to go ahead and happen for more people to awaken. Before the shift and the domino effect can take place. We understand that there are people who are feeling like they're sitting on the edge just waiting for the word 'go' so they can jump off this planet, but there needs to be more people really ready and willing to do that before we can go ahead with anything further.

J: What can we do to help assist those people to be more ready?

K: Again, there are things that are going to happen. There are things that are taking place now that are helping those people. There is nothing other than what you and many other people are doing now that can help force anyone awake. People are coming across YouTube videos and information in their own way that is helping them awaken. People are being triggered, and it's those triggers that are causing those people to come across information that is helping them awaken. Every day there are more and more people. It's like light bulbs are turning on all over the place above people's heads, if you know what I mean.

J: Getting epiphanies.

K: That's right, exactly, so we need to let more of that happen. It's happening so much faster, it's happening so much easier, that those low vibrational people that are trying to prevent it from happening are starting to panic. We can see them pushing the panic buttons because we are going to experience something amazing, and they're going to lose power. But we just need to wait a bit more.

J: So it truly is up to individuals who are here on this planet to step up, raise their vibrations, and be of service?

K: Yes, but they can't be forced. We all just need to be patient. They will awaken at their own pace. But like we said, it's happening so much faster by the masses already. But we just need more, there's billions and billions of people on this planet. And millions and millions are awakening every day. But millions are still taking a while. So we just need to be patient and enjoy what it is on Earth that you have now, because it's going to be different when we get there. Does that make sense?

J: But it's not going to be different in a bad way. It's just going to be quite profoundly different.

K: It's going to be amazing, it's just nothing like we have experienced here on Earth.

J: Thank you so much, are there any final messages you would like us to know?

K: Don't get frustrated, not just you, but people don't get frustrated waiting — because the frustration is causing people to forget what it is that they're here to do. The shift will happen when it happens. Just enjoy your experiences now. And for those holding on to karma, they need to release it. There's nothing further.

J: Okay, thank you, and while we can accept everyone's on their own journey and pace, those people who are still refusing to look at the inner work, when they've been almost told about it daily, us having patience and tolerance and understanding and compassionate love towards them, while not disempowering them or enabling them. It becomes quite challenging to know the difference and how to support people the most, when they're not wanting to even support themselves.

K: Put it this way: the only time we can shake someone awake, well, we can't, but the only time someone can be shaken awake is when tragedy strikes. You have people talking about their life and death experiences after a bad accident. When they come back, they talk about that experience, and they become very spiritual, very open-minded and a different person, physical person. Some people will need that tragic tragedy or some sort of trigger to happen for them to awaken, and that's okay. Some people will have a simple near-death experience where they're about to cross the road, and a car almost hits them, and that is a trigger that they will have. Some people will see a video on YouTube and that will be a trigger. And some people will simply hear a sentence, perhaps in the background, or in a YouTube video that they watch, or something that they see, and that will be there to trigger. Everyone will have different triggers, but they will have them. We just need to be patient and let them experience that at their own pace.

J: Thank you, thank you very much.

To listen to the 10 sessions as they were given,

the playlist:

"Moving from 3D to 5D series"

can be found on the YOUTUBE channel

Conversation with Heaven on Earth

Summary Session

"It is time to awaken!" "You have a mission! It is time to begin!" "Stop wasting time! Time is growing short for you to accomplish what you came to Earth to do!"

~~~~~~~~~~~~~~~~~~

As a second wave volunteer, knowing more about my life purpose and contract from the dozens of sessions I have had as a QHHT and BQH client, I knew I could do more. So I merged sessions with other practitioners and many clients around the world to create these books MASTERING OLD EARTH, MASTERING HUMAN, and now this guide for all practitioners to encourage them to explore this important concept about what the shift to New Earth actually is meaning for most people. Two coming books which are in the editing stage as this is being published are: Time: The Convoluted Concept of Being Human and Depressed People Don't Eat Salads.

The following session was done in 2021, and while we are still getting the same information from clients who have never heard any sessions we have shared publicly, this is another set of questions to explore for the most curious of practitioners and clients. For the next book a team of us will publish, we will be exploring these questions again to compare what new information our collectives would like us to learn.

Arcturian and Pleiadian Collectives, Their Message to You
(2021)

J: I'd like to call upon the collectives of the Arcturians and the Pleiadians, because I have some questions.

V: Yes, we are here at this moment.

J: Thank you very much. Can you explain to us how you are here, and how we came to meet with you today?

V: We can connect with you because, for one, you have used your free will to ask for the connection and sought the connection. We provide transmissions all throughout your lives, and it is when you truly ask with free will to heighten those transmissions and to connect, that we really are able to provide that. But everything in where we are at is energy — and so that energy that we are a part of, we are able to transmit into a way that gets into a field within your realm that creates the connection. It's all just frequency and energy, how we transmit this information. Then the vehicle that is transmitting the information, portrays our information in their words, or slang or the provided text through grammar that we provide them.

J: So you're using her body to be able prompt her voice to speak your messages?

V: Yes, we are portraying it in what relates to her, so that she can relay the information. So when she has stepped back in this hypnotic state, we are able to then kind of hijack the frequency, hijack the channel if you will, and be able to provide you our pure message, where the ego is not, the vehicle is not, a part of the message.

J: From your perspective, what is a hypnotic state? Because so many people think that it is dangerous and evil.

V: The hypnotic state is just a brainwave state that allows the ego to step back, and it allows the information. It's just like a radio channel. It allows us to have clear communication on that radio channel. Instead of where you get when you're in between two radio channels, and it's a fuzzy channel, where you're getting two different radio frequencies, and you're kind of hearing two types of music on an FM transmitter — it's just like that. So, it is a brainwave state where the ego steps back, and we have a clear channel.

J: Thank you, there are two Facebook groups we support: "New Earth Information - Dolores Cannon" and "Arcturian and Pleiadian Starseeds". Both are growing in great numbers. As you have already said in a few sessions, how is this purposeful for the collectives to have us come together? Why now? Why do you want us to create Facebook groups to support these starseeds?

V: Well, because just the same as we had covered in the last session, it's about providing support for the ones that were crying out through these sessions. There were also others, you know. We were not able to reach all with those sessions that we would like. So this is another capability for the ones that are confused, and the ones that have unknowingly, in no malice or no judgment, but have been using more resources with their confusion and

the SHIFT to NEW EARTH

their desire for help. This is another avenue where we can provide support, information, clear and direct information to our collectives. These are our soldiers on the ground, if you will, and we could parallel it to like a military command that provides support and structure and correct information. Pure information has been, as you know, all over the place, with the information integrity on other groups, based on the channeling that the other groups were getting. So we were wanting to provide our support for our troops on the ground. This method is truly the message through the clear channeling that we could provide.

J: Is there a problem with channeling that isn't pure?

V: There are people who are able to channel, but they're only able to channel where their ego isn't stepping back. And so you know where ego is, what it is, but when you have two conflicting frequencies providing information — then you are not getting the highest information. So this is a source where the ego is stepped back and the support that is in the hierarchy at the top — they are very clear in pure channelings. So it is not one where ego kind of fuzzies that vibration and that information that is received through the group.

J: How can you, how can humans, how can people know the difference between a channeling that has ego and a channeling that doesn't?

V: Well, people can use their free will to ask their teams, and it won't resonate. It won't feel right. It will feel like it just feels wrong in your gut. You all have the capabilities to use your free will to ask if anything provided in your life is of true or false frequency. You could look at it from the point of, does this look like ego? Does this look like something that someone's using a platform to gain financially, or to boost themselves and make themselves feel better? When the ego is not stepped back, that's when you know you're not getting the purest source of information.

J: But for those people who can't trust their guts and are still looking for outside information and confirmation, there is a disconnect from people still trusting their intuition. What can they do to help navigate through that?

V: Well, they can use their free will to ask for that connection to be more pure within themselves. Grounding is huge. It's huge in creating the connections and the circuitry connections within the chakras which are receptors to information and energy around you. That is when you have blockages and you're not grounded and you don't have that water to conduct all of those signals — it does create a disconnect in the intuition because there's not flow within all the circuitry in the body.

J: So, water is important for grounding, what else?

V: The consumption of what you put into your body with thoughts. If you're putting negative thoughts in your body, if you're putting negative information and everything that you see. What you put in your body as far as the density of the food that it provides for your body — all these things can lower your frequency, and that will provide a less pure channel.

J: I see, okay, we thank you so much. Why are people afraid of other species, for example, yourselves, the Pleiadians and Arcturians? What's going on there?

V: Well, the thought of us physically is something that naturally would put you into fear. Because it's just like you get startled by something that is unknown. It's also the narrative that's been played throughout time, and the history of the ill intent or abductions, and not looking at it from the bigger picture of life contracts. That has all been indoctrinated into your subconscious, and people fear the unknown and the information of that. They've had to rely on something other than them. It has also created a disconnect and understanding that we all should trust and know when we see something that's of difference. Is this to harm me or is this to help me? People still have a disconnect with their inner trust of the fact that if we chose and we wanted to have harmed and take over the world, we would have done it by now. We are here in love and support of all, and only want to help humanity. Looking at the higher perspective, that would really help people out, but they have had such closed-minded thinking in a lot of ways, and that is just because of the systems that were set up to keep people in cycles and fear.

J: Thank you, and so for those people who are questioning, how could you love us and be here for us when humanity is going through such horrible, say for example, the crimes against humanity, how has that been allowed to occur?

V: Well, the crimes against humanity have happened

because there were things put in place on Earth, there were rules that were supposed to be followed. There were life contracts of others that would be looked at as lower density sources or negative energy sources per humanity's eyes that were fulfilling life contracts to allow people to use their free will to ascend the karmic ladder to enlightenment. However, things did go astray, and there were people who just didn't want to. It got out of hand, and then humanity got stuck here within the cycles and was not able to leave the Earth grid. It became somewhat of a downward spiral. So, we have sent our troops, both collectives, here, that are with us now. We have sent our troops to help, our light workers to help and assist. We've sent energy frequencies within the Earth to help assist within the awakening, so that we could evacuate all that wanted to evacuate and go to where they chose to go to honor their contracts and to free this karmic cycle that has entrapped and enslaved humanity.

J: Thank you so much, and we really appreciate that you are assisting us with this. What do you want us to understand and know about other beings that people are very afraid of? How are we supposed to understand the purpose of the reptilians and their agenda?

V: You're supposed to understand that not all are bad, and in ways that even that you would perceive it, that there are just a few bad apples, and the rest are just like you. You guys all have a few bad apples within your systems that humanity has set up, and the rest are just people who have wanted to live their lives. They're just beings who just wanted to honor their contract and live the life that they wanted to live. We say, unfortunately, as a way for humanity to understand, but, unfortunately, the few bad apples have ruined it for the rest. It is not hard for us to love you because we are all from energy Source. We are all from unity Source. We are all light. We are all love. You all have forgotten who you are. You all have forgotten what your purpose is here and your contract and what you wanted to experience in those dense times. The dense energies, it can feel like something is out to get you, but when you look at it with a new focus and a new understanding that everything is love and light, and that we are all just working on this together, you will then lose the fear narrative and realize how much you actually have empowerment and you know what the future looks like for yourself.

J: Can we ask for all the Pleiadian and Arcturians collectives to be able to send profound energy to all of their starseeds who are listening to this, at this time, for them to be able to notice the frequency and activate them so they can start remembering who they are now?

V: Yes, we will send that right now. We are showing the vehicle a white light of just energy being sent out and being connected and just that powerful energy that people will feel within their bodies. We are helping them remember. This is so important to remember who you are. **Remember the strength that you have, and remember that you are all love. You are all love and light.**

J: Is it helpful for people to remember their other past lifetimes, so then they realize that this is just merely one experience that they need to overcome and be of service to?

V: It is helpful for people to learn the details of their past lives, but it is also just helpful for them to understand that they have past, future and present lives all happening. Maybe the details at this point are not going to help so much, but just the general understanding that there is what you would call 'reincarnation', and there are purposes and lessons that you learn through each and every lifetime. The next lifetime, what would be perceived as past this ascension, is going to be beautiful and filled with unity and love and laughter and joy and freedom. There is so much freedom, and maybe not to dwell so much in the past, but to look forward to the future. Realize that you have the power to move towards that future, and just ask your team, just ask for that connection.

J: Thank you, so for those people who are stuck with the density of knowing about, for example, the crimes against humanity, what are they supposed to do with the information? How are they supposed to process it?

V: Well, they need to heal. They need to realize that that has already happened, that there's nothing they can do to change the contracts of those that were all affected by crimes against humanity, and that it has already happened. So to go back in time, and to take yourself to that energy frequency of that time is doing nothing to serve you today. Today, look at the bigger picture, that there had to be an awakening to free humanity from the enslavement within the cycles. With that information, honor it and say 'thank you' to all who chose to come here and endure that. 'I honor you, and I want to apply these lessons to my daily lives in the present moment and move forward to a better future.'

J: Fantastic, and in terms of this vehicle, this transmission, we have discovered that her Subconscious is an Arcturian. Is that correct? (V: Yes) Thank you, and so even though we know she's had many other lifetimes with different starseeds, could you say that not just the Arcturian collective are supporting her, but all of her other soul family members? How would you like us to understand that?

V: So when you visit in past lifetimes, she has been to other planetary systems, and she picked up the energy frequency of the collectives that inhabited those planetary systems. It stays with you. This energy frequency, although predominantly Arcturian, she has energy frequencies of other collectives. Those other collectives can then use their transmissions to support and to help the vehicle in her journey. So no, it is not just one collective that supports her. It's almost like you're a collector of collectives, if that makes sense. You go around, you have this empty bag, and wherever you visit in your lifetimes — you're collecting the energy frequency, and you put that in your bag. So now you have transmission capabilities to be able to communicate and support, and her collective predominantly likes to gather data. They like to provide that, but there are other collectives that are gathering different types of data. When they need to kind of get a download of all of their troops on the fields, they say, 'okay, upload this to us with this information,' and she can upload that information to help the collectives for whatever they're supporting within the planetary system.

J: Thank you, and could it be true to say that different collectives get different information regarding the future plans for this Earth?

V: They do get different information; some collectives work more closely with others. Some are here just for a different purpose. Some are here as really just observers, and they're really not doing a lot with that data. They're just observing. Some are applying that data and looking at outcomes and fine-tuning the information, then how they steer their collectives. There are a lot of different purposes for different collectives for watching humanity and watching what's happening on planet Gaia right now. It just depends on where they're at and their roles of what they want to achieve as to what is transmitted to them.

J: Thank you, and so for people who are wondering about ascension symptoms, what's happening to their bodies? Why are they finding it hard to sleep, and why do they have ringing in the ears? Can you explain to people who haven't really heard it directly from yourselves what is going on here?

V: Well, there are a lot of things going on, and we'll touch base on some of them to help provide clarity. The main thing is right now, if you look at it as your periodic table of elements — you are a carbon-based body, and with the ascension, what needs to happen is: some will go to pure energy and some will go to a crystalline source of energy for their body. And so, you will not have the same carbon body. And a lot of the energy that we are providing to this Earth right now is upgrading and reactivating the DNA which they have called dormant DNA, to upgrade to a crystalline body. And that has to happen and like when you are a child and you are growing bigger — you get growing pains, you get lethargic. It's a very hard time when all that energy is producing and changing and the cells are multiplying and pulling apart and upgrading, and that can create a lot of the physical symptoms. However, the group that is primarily that this session is focused on are also a lot of the starseeds on the Earth right now. You guys are all intercepting that energy that we are infusing up into the system, and you guys are all transmuting that, changing it, working with it. There's a huge amount of energy change that's helping, also, for the things that have been toxic to the bodies on Earth that humanity has been subjected to throughout time, including the drastic DNA changes through breeding programs. We are providing all this to just basically change the cells within your body and the energy around you, to help heighten the frequency, help keep people high vibration, and to help assist in the ascension.

J: Can you explain to people what the ascension is?

V: The ascension encompasses all: mind, body and soul. And that includes the soul, mind, and body of this planetary system, what we refer to as Gaia. Humanity is going through a huge ascension to the fifth dimension. And that is a fifth dimensional mindset, that is a fifth dimensional physical body. And not all will go to a 5D planet — we want to be very clear about that. But there is a majority that will, that choose to, in their life contract, ascend to New Earth. This is just a way for us to awaken the body, the mind, and the soul to prepare for that. Because the 3D mindsets and the lower density energies and feelings and emotions and behaviors cannot exist on the 5D planet. We are loosening all that and releasing it so that once the ascension happens, it will be left behind like a weight.

J: For those people who are scared because they are starting to question, does that mean that they have to die to shift to the fifth dimension? What would you like them to know?

V: That does not mean you have to die, but some people have chosen in their life contract that that is their way of passing. They knew they were coming into this denseness within this world, and they said, 'okay, I can handle it to a point, but I don't want to be pushed further than that,' and that's fine. That was their limit, their threshold of what they wanted to experience within this experience on planet Earth. We honor the life contract, and they pass, and they ascend. However, the ones that that does not happen to, that is not a death — it is actually a rebirth in a way, or actually for once, living in a way that it was truly essentially supposed to be, without the cyclic behaviors.

J: For those people who have experienced someone dying and struck with grief, can you explain to them what those feelings of grief are?

V: Those feelings of grief are something you put on yourself — because we are not taught the bigger picture of a reincarnation on this Earth, for the most part. There are some that are awakened to it. Grief is that release of some of those sticking things within that lower density emotion or energy that you have in it. Grief can be a vibration to help to unstick that, as long as you move through it, and don't stay in it. When you stay in it, it becomes another cycle that you have put yourself in. Grief can be very profoundly healing, as long as you empower yourself to honor it and to allow it to move and not stay in it — is the most important thing. Because we see a lot of humanity just gets stuck in the storytelling of the grief, and that just places you in another place and time in the past, instead of in the present moment.

J: Thank you, in terms of this vehicle, she's had many other lifetimes. How many other physical bodies has she had?

V: We are showing her three.

J: When you're having these lifetimes, you must instantly and naturally feel very attached to the body?

V: You can be, but you can also disconnect that. The body is something of comfort. It is like, what we've described before, it's like a weighted blanket. It feels very comfortable, it's very nice to move in, and it is something that is a new experience for some. It is very exciting to not just be energy, in a way, but to be something of a denseness. However, this vehicle is very excited for her crystalline body and says she won't miss it too much.

J: Fantastic, and when she does shift into her crystalline body, will she experience any discomfort or pain?

V: No, she will not experience discomfort or pain at all. It's just a lifting, it's just a lightness. When the disconnect happens, it is just like when you're falling asleep almost, and you just kind of drift away — that's what it's going to feel like. We have fine-tuned the way of disconnecting that will not harm or create trauma to anybody that is going to experience that.

J: Fantastic, and when she's in her crystalline body and she gets to the New Earth, how would she view her life there on the New Earth?

V: She will view it as just such a purpose. She's very excited to go. She is going to help humanity with that transition. She's already been provided imagery of this New Earth before, and she says it's just a wonderful, beautiful place. Watching everyone interact in such a different way of love centered, it's just so refreshing for her to even look forward to. She looks forward to reconnecting with her soul family there, and she looks forward to the freedom. As much as you want to create a free mindset within this lower density Earth, it's very hard to live that way because of all the things that the lower energies and frequencies that are impacting you to have that. She's really looking forward to the liberation and freedom that she has seen on New Earth before.

J: Wonderful, okay, well, thank you so much. So why now, why are we hearing about this shift now? Why does it have to occur?

V: It has to occur because the vessel within Gaia, what humanity has done to her vessel, not only the human DNA vessels and the reprogramming of the bodies — there is no way to undo what has happened. The toxicity with even Gaia's waters — it's just been taken over, and so we had to come up with a plan to liberate all. And it is not just humanity, there are other beings within planet

Earth that are being affected by this as well. They have collectives, and they've been calling out to their collectives. So we've all come together to assist, to liberate all that are here, so that they can now move forward to a new place, a new vessel.

J: So we understand that we're talking to the Pleiadian and the Arcturian collectives. Can you give us a sense of how many other collectives are here helping humanity and this planet at this time, and all the beings here?

V: We're showing her 144, and she doesn't know if that's the thousand or if that's the number of collectives.

J: I see, we've just recently seen the discussion of the 144,000 volunteers. There are bible references to it, and there's a lot of people saying it's chosen people. What would you like us to know about that?

V: Well they are not chosen people, although some did get voluntold[19]. They are beings that came using their free will, wanting to have an experience, and to help assist with the frequency. That is not a physical number of the exact amount, that is the amount that are supporting the people down there. It is the star systems and the soul sparks, it is the supporters, the number of the supporters of all — there are much more than 144,000 within the realm of Gaia right now.

J: Okay, well, thank you so much. So there's all those collectives that are helping, which is extraordinary. We

---

[19] When souls were expected to come and help over simply volunteering, they were told to come.

really appreciate that. In terms of the toxicity in the waters, can you give me an update of what the water is like now for those that drink the water?

V: The water in city pipelines and what government officials put in their water, and well, most of the water within Gaia, whether it be ocean water or lake water — it is just riddled with toxicity. There is nuclear waste. There's dumpage within the water. There are man-made artificial things put within your water to make you sick, to control you, to create a disconnect. The fluoride in your water creates a disconnect within your pineal gland and calcifies other chakras — to not allow you to have pure transmissions. And water is memory, and if you think of the toxicity of the memory within the water — that has been also a crime against humanity, that they couldn't awaken. The veil was harder to remove because they were consuming things that naturally dulled down the memory of what this planetary system was supposed to experience and how it was supposed to be a wonderful place.

J: In many of your sessions, the information you give us is to drink water, so how are we to trust that the water that we're drinking isn't going to harm us?

V: Well, there are ways to choose a more pure source of a natural water to do that. But the main thing is that you guys are powerful creators. You guys are powerful beings. You put your loving hands around that water and you just put healing intentions and loving intentions within that water — that alone, even though you may not see it, the energy frequency that you are transmitting into that water is manifesting a pure source of love in memory and a remembrance that you can use your free will to create that safety within your water.

J: Okay, and so how important is drinking water at the moment?

V: It's one of the most important things you could do, besides going within, because it helps the transmissions within your cells for the memory and the activation of everything that we're trying to help you with right now.

J: For those people who've never heard the term 'going within', what does it actually mean? How do people do that practically?

V: Going within is a way that you can connect to your center. It's a way that you can go within, and you can connect to us. It's to shut out the external interferences, and when you go within, you can feel that you're within yourself. You're within alignment. You're within your heart. It is to create a kind of a silence to the outside world and that allows us then to give you an understanding and a connection and a communication that is not distorted by the outside world. Once you master this, you're able to do it on a more frequent basis where you don't have to necessarily study at it or sit still with it. Once the connection happens, there becomes a healing within that. And as long as you keep a constant connection with us, you then can go about your day. You don't have to be just silent. Everything you do can have a connection with us. It's just for those that have forgotten or have had alterations to the ability to be able to connect, that it does have to be as somewhat of an intentional, very mindful practice at first.

J: For those people who have things that are blocking them from connecting to their spiritual team, to yourselves, to go within — are we able to ask that this block be removed from them today? As they ask their free will to be connected back to their teams profoundly, are we able to assist them with this?

V: Yes, but the important thing is: we'd like all to ask with their free will, and to start realizing that they have free will to ask for all. It's very important in this journey for people to realize how powerful their free will is. They are on a free will planet. Although we'd like to come in, and we'd like to shake you, and say, 'okay, we're just going to make this connection happen,' we rarely do that because that goes against the laws of what we're able to do. It is so important we can provide these and leave these transmissions out there, but humanity needs to get accustomed to asking with their free will. You guys have mastered doomsday free will in your lives just fine. But you guys haven't mastered and realize the manifestation of using your free will for the good stuff and creating that reality. It's really important for that because that will be something that you can take with you to New Earth, and it will be part of the lessons there.

J: If humanity all got together and set the intentions to heal Gaia and clean her body so it wasn't toxic, what would happen then?

V: Unfortunately, it wouldn't happen. There are some laws within this realm that you cannot bypass. Although humanity would want to do that and the intention, what it would do was create a connection of that unity of all thinking for a higher purpose — and that is a lesson that is very good for taking on to the New Earth. However, what has happened to Gaia's vessel and what is in Gaia's contract — we cannot violate Gaia's free will. Gaia has already decided she is moving on, and as much as humanity would want to do that, you cannot violate her free will.

J: Thank you, yes, I understand. Getting back to the people who are trying to give information about starseeds and our life purposes and trying to life coach people — wouldn't one of the biggest things that they should be trying to do is to empower others by saying what you've already said to us today about going within and seeking your own information, rather than relying on others who are paying for that service?

V: Yes. We can provide all to you when you have that true connection. Anything you seek — we can provide. That is a faith that humanity needs to have within themselves and with us, that we want to only help humanity, the starseeds, the light workers, whatever you guys want to call yourself. We are only here to help you guys, and you have to help yourself at some point. It is a free will planet. You have to ask for that help. Those other types of information for the newly awakened ones can be a pathway and a help, but that can't be the source of information because it is external. External information is only supposed to be a small tool until you realize how powerful you are, that you don't need the external information, and that your information comes from within.

J: I know there's people that are listening that are very literal, and so what would be the magic words that they would have to say to be able to get the support and attention of their guides to know they want more information, they want more access, they want more communication?

V: Well, when you go to telepathy, you have to realize that your intentions and your words have to match, and whatever it is for you, that your intention and your words match. There's so many different options of things you could say, but your intention and what your heart is aligning to, what you truly want — you use that and you use your words, or however you communicate. If you want to do telepathy, you do that in alignment. Then it won't matter what the words are, because we'll know you're asking for that help.

J: And again, it goes back to those people who are afraid of other beings because they may be ETs or monsters.

V: You guys are all ETs.

J: Indeed, okay, thank you. Yes, we get it, and in terms of people being afraid of inoculations changing people's DNA, what would you like us to know about that?

V: Well, once again if you're in fear with it, I would ask what that fear is? Where does that attach to? Ask us for help in helping you guide that, and realize that these are life contracts. People knew, the souls that came into this world that are choosing to do this, they knew what they were signing up for. They knew this was a part of their life contract, and they have worked closely with their teams in dream states to align this to happen. When you are in fear of somebody making a choice for themselves — that doesn't empower you very much. Look at it as an honor and a gratitude that they are here having this experience alongside you on this beautiful planet. Yes, it changes DNA, but change is not such a bad thing when you're ascending to a 5D planet. Change has to occur. Change is happening all around you, so if you fear change — it's because you're blocking, and you're resisting the energy flow within yourself at some point. I would ask: where is that blockage that I have, that I am in fear or in doubt or worried about this? Because it's more or less about something that's going on with you, within you, than it is about the other person having the freedom to make their own choice.

J: Fantastic, and for those people who have experiences of being possessed, what would you like us to know about that?

V: Well, I mean for one, we redirect everything that's a part of your life contract, that you chose to have that experience. The experience of being possessed is just a lower density energy, that lower frequency. When we look at everything with energy and frequency, it's just, I mean, listen, we're going to be very blunt. The crimes against humanity, there's all kinds of controlling things that have happened to you, and you've all been possessed in one way or another, by lower frequency energy, to harm one another. A possession is just like a physical manifestation of that. It's there to create a decision and a pathway of a choice. For some people, they need that to wake up. They need that to redirect. Their teams have provided that experience because they were going down a path that wasn't honoring their contract. They had the free will then, after that, to ask questions, and to seek it, and to understand it, and to maybe make different choices that rerouted them back to their contract. But if you look at everything that has a purpose with a life contract, it's easy to sit kind of in a command station and realize how those things could very well help recourse people to a better place that they wanted to experience. It doesn't have to be just doom and gloom.

J: For those people who are still reacting to things as doom and gloom, what are your messages for them?

V: Our messages are to ask for us to release that for you, to constantly do things that make you feel more empowered and increase your vibration. The doom and gloom is something you are self-feeding yourself. You have the choice whether you want to experience those things or not. And be very, very careful of the things that you put into your body with your mind, the things you watch, the things you say to yourself, the stories you tell, because those stories are something you're feeding yourself. It is a direct mirror of things that you are saying in your head. And we want to empower you to ask your teams to help assist you, to help align those blockages, to help free you and release and alchemize that energy that's within you — because it's all just perception. The perception is something you're placing on yourself.

J: A lot of our systems place labels on ourselves. The medical industry is very good at doing that. What would you like us to understand about that?

V: For some, it can be a journey of just finding that knowledge and finding ways to support, depending on what it is, to then find solutions to it. And that can help bring higher vibrational solutions. For some, they live within those labels. Those labels become the defining part of them. You are not born into this world with a label. That is something that is placed on you — whether it be by self or by an external source. So if that label is something that's to propel you to a solution — then that's fine. We say it was very purposeful. But once again about the cycles within humanity, if that label is something that you just want to wear, you want to get that label tattooed on you now because you like that label so much, it's now just going to become one with you. You get that label tattooed, and that is the defining marker of who you are. Well, what is that really serving? You're just staying stuck in a cycle. That isn't moving forward, that's just disempowering you. We tell humanity: labels can be purposeful, but they can also serve the lower density energies. They can also keep you stuck in a cycle that is not serving you, and it's not serving humanity.

J: Right, okay, well, thank you. We've been hearing about some solar flares that are gonna come and put energy onto the planet. What would you like us to know and understand about that, please?

V: Well, there are solar flares that have been happening, and they have happened throughout time. They are increasing, and they're a tool we use to help penetrate the fields around Gaia right now, and to activate certain energy fields and energy vortexes that we need to activate to help humanity. It is also something that will be a part of the release of the carbon body of Gaia, in all of the humanity that is releasing, and it will activate the crystalline bodies. So it is all very purposeful. It is something that is increasing, and it does create natural disasters, the fields, when it is penetrated into Gaia. But it is all very purposeful, and it releases that dense energy. A lot of humanity do feel them, and they're very susceptible to them, but that is just them processing and alchemizing the energy and releasing the denseness.

J: Thank you so much. We understand that there is a lot of disinformation going around, including from many starseed families. What would you like us to know today about Nesara and Gesara and the financial resets?

V: We want you to know that if you're fixated on not having to worry about money — you have a lot more inner work to do, because when this happens, money's not going to be an issue, whether this activates or not. So if your focus is money, I would question the source, and I would question why it's so important. If you're living your day-to-day lives and moving forward and trusting that everything will be provided for you, then Nesara and Gesara are just a distraction. And so we ask you, why do you need this distraction right now when it is so much more imperative to do your inner work? So if anything that you're listening or attuning to within yourself or within an outside source is based upon 3D materialistic things — we would suggest that you go within and ask to be released of that 3D grounded mindset, and to ground yourself more in a 5D mindset of higher things because where you're going — money is not going to be needed.

J: Well, what do you say to the people who are fixated on the politics and the systems there? Is there going to be a reset? For those people who are still focused on politics and what is happening, what would you like them to know?

V: Well, just like anything else, are you using it just to observe and to look at and get a higher enlightened understanding? Or are you surrounding yourself in it and stuck in that cycle? So if anything is not empowering, as far as the information, is it a tool and a method to gather data and see what's going on and to see how humanity's going? But am I going to stay stuck there and just be stuck in that cycle? Everything that you do, I would look at: is this helping empower me, and am I flowing through it? Am I just observing, or am I using it as a way to define or to keep myself within a cycle?

J: Thank you so much, and for those people who are aware of all the crimes against humanity, and are very awake to all of the corrupt systems, and they still cannot manage to see the bigger perspective. Can you just once again remind them how they're supposed to process that information, and have it from a bigger perspective?

V: Yes, process it, that this was their life contract. This is what was needed to empower and awaken humanity. That had this not occurred, that humanity would be stuck in very, very, what you would term, sick cycles and oppressive cycles, lower frequency cycles. We want you to focus on the empowerment and honor, and you can give gratitude to those who came and endured that. It's very beautiful to send them healing and to send them love, but empower yourself now to be the change within yourself. Don't let their experience go wasted by wasting your life and being stuck in those experiences. Honor them by doing your role that you wanted to perform here within this realm. Honor them by going within and releasing childhood traumas, releasing hurdles, giving yourself love. That love will flow to others. Honor the cycles that have had to happen so that we can move forward to a better place of enlightenment, of love, of support for one another, and so that this never happens again. But we can't move forward without that healing, and I just empower you to heal.

J: Thank you so much, and from your perspective, being high dimensional beings, and you have seen and been aware of all that is happening to this planet, can we trust that we can just focus on our own inner work, knowing that there are higher dimensional beings supporting all?

V: We've got you. We have nothing but love for you all and for all the beings that inhabit during this time and in the past, present, and future. We are nothing but love, so the best thing that you can do is trust. Trust is a very hard thing for humanity. And you have to trust in the bigger plan. Trust that you are part of that plan. Your part in that plan is you have to trust yourself — that you have the answers. Trust that you doing the inner work, that you moving forward, that it is all part of the bigger plan that we need you to do, and we are trusting you to do. So we are all trusting one another and loving one another, in this whole plan in the ascension that's going on right now.

J: Thank you. Could you say it's accurate that the whole other agenda that has been going on for humanity is to distrust themselves and to distrust others and be afraid?

V: The whole agenda right now is separation. There's a lot of things that you're taught throughout your lifetime that you're separated from. You're taught that you're separated from Source. That you are subservient to Source in many religions. You're taught that you are separated from love, you're separated from family, you're separated from peers all the time. This agenda that has always gone on within humanity is just a cyclic recycling of the separation— especially this past year; standing six feet apart, putting a mask on, can't see a smile of your neighbor — that's separation. And even though the technology of the internet does have its purpose, and it does create support, it also creates separation. That you can hide behind your ego. With all these filters they put on cameras that you have to be something else other than what you are — that's separation from self. So all these crimes against humanity and especially this past year have taught us to be nothing but fearful and separate from one another, when really what we're moving towards is unity love. We're never supposed to be separate. We are always supposed to understand our part in it and how we have a ripple effect with one another, how we could help one another. This has all just been a part of that, but we are seeing that it's actually causing the awakening within others, when they're saying "No more, I love my neighbor," and they're not reacting in the ways that they were programmed to react.

J: In terms of your relationship with each other, the Pleiadians and the Arcuturians, what would you like us to understand and know today?

V: Well, we want to provide to you that we are working

together, and we are helping support our collectives, our starseeds that are on the ground right now. We do provide different information for our collectives, and we do share some information. Some information we are just figuring out, and sometimes we do have disconnects in the information that we provide. However, we try to be as much of a unified source as possible, because there are other collectives that really don't work with us as much. We know that we're stronger together.

J: Thank you so much. For those people who have listened to this and are worried and concerned that they have family members who don't understand what is happening to Gaia or what's happening to humanity, it is true that they do not need to know or even believe about this or be aware of this information for it to still happen for them and for them to shift? Is that correct?

V: That's correct. There are some that will be completely asleep before the ascension, and that is part of the purpose. That is part of the contract. We have resources in what we will utilize to help them along the journey, on the ships, to be able to upgrade them and prepare them and to get them back online, if you will. However, with how the Earth is right now and all the systems of control, there have been some that we have had to put our focus on. The ones that we've needed to put our focus on and that is especially our starseeds on this Earth for the awakening. Because we know that you all have a role and a purpose with this ascension, once the shift happens. You guys will have jobs to do, so it is very important for us to keep you guys online and help you guys through your inner work, so that we can utilize you within the ascension of the ones that are completely asleep.

J: So the purpose of the awakening, can you give us your definition of that?

V: Well, the veil is lifting, that is the awakening. The lifting of the veil and the reconnection within your bodies.

J: I see. Fantastic, okay, so we know that there are going to be epic times ahead for humanity as this shift is occurring. Until that time, what would you like people to focus on the most?

V: Focus on the present now. Whatever you feel resistance to — work on that. Ask for healing, flow through it. We want you to raise your vibration, connect with Gaia, connect with the sun, connect with the ground, connect with one another, connect with your heart and love one another. Everything that you need to experience will be placed in your path. You don't have to go searching for it. So have trust and have faith in that. Keep moving forward. When you get stuck, ask your team for help, and it's all going to be okay.

J: Thank you, we really appreciate the information you've provided for us today because it gives us great clarification, and we understand. For those people who still are not too sure about the purpose of the Arcturians and the Pleiadians, they needed to sit with themselves and just really feel into whether they can trust this or not. Can we send profound love and healing to those people who still can't trust themselves, because I know that's a big step forward? Most people can't trust themselves, so they can't really distinguish what their inner gut feeling is. I've seen this and heard this many times, where people are trying to connect in, but because they don't trust themselves, they get misinformation, and it really flips the script of what they really should be aware of.

V: We can send that healing, and we would love to. Remember, you guys have all had this programming that has been placed within your systems — and you can reprogram that. You are the creator of what that programming is. The more you trust, the more you reprogram those past stories that do not serve you and have only enslaved you. So when you think of it like that, don't you want out of slavery? Don't you want freedom? And you have to trust. That has to be something that you can only do within yourself. We will help support, and we will help provide the healing, if you ask us. But you have to trust us and trust yourself because ultimately — you are the healer, because you are the ones using your free will to trust and to seek healing.

J: Thank you so much for your love and your wisdom and your support. I know it has helped so many to be able to navigate through the density of the emotions and to be able to provide them inspiration to do their inner work to release them from things that no longer served them.

V: You're very welcome, and we just want to tell you all that we love you so much. We are so proud of you. Be proud of yourselves! This was a brave contract of service that you came into. Be proud, and do not resist the change in the flow to a better place. New Earth awaits you all!

the SHIFT to NEW EARTH

J: Very inspirational, thank you so much!

Farewell note

Our collectives, guides, Subconscious, soul family, Arcturians, higher self, over soul, Angels, Source — whatever you want to call THEM — they are HERE TO HELP US. Do not be shy asking them about anything. There are truly no small or too personal questions that they cannot help with. They want to help us and that is part of their life contract with us. When we honor and respect their advice, we can advance quickly. It can take some time to trust them. When we are left confused about a concept, we can easily distrust them, over remembering we are still using our human minds to understand advanced information.

Exploring the concept of time with these sessions is very convoluted, and we have been asked to create an entirely new book about this which is coming next — that is called <u>Time: The Convoluted Concept of Being Human</u>. It is still a work in process, but we are being given more information they want us to add into this for you to explore.

Everything that is physical has a beginning and an end — and there are only so many timeline branches we can explore before the official OLD EARTH experience unfolds as it needs to. We were asked to create <u>Mastering Old Earth</u>, which you can also read from Quantum sessions.

the SHIFT to NEW EARTH

We have been seeing people shifting for years, and we keep hearing people cannot reincarnate on Earth again for a very long time after the density has been cleansed. They are saying we can understand this length of time as being EONS, hence why we are hearing souls will shift to New Earth or return to other home planets, go and heal with Source, or return to another 3D planet for a softer experience to be able to complete all that the souls want to complete in 3D.

If we have life contracts to shift to New Earth, we still need to work towards that. We are not just given this free pass if our frequency energy is too dense. If we are meant to be of service to others on New Earth — we are in training for this now, as there is much support needed for those who will be very confused about what is happening to them and their family.

Doing our own inner work is not just extremely helpful and provides inner peace for ourselves, but also to all who are around us and for the human conscious collectives also. While we are living here on Earth, we are all part of humanity and our collective mindsets, which can be called Christ Consciousness — which empowers ALL here when each of us grow, while playing the role of being human.

Enjoy your sessions. Deeply relax into them, knowing this is THEIR information, over your own opinions. The more you practice with being clients and practitioners, the more at ease you will be asking the big questions and be able to apply all the information given. Listening to them is important, and if you have any confusion — go back with more questions, and explore as many clients as you can to learn more about who can shift to the New Earth, and which collective beings are still working their way towards a 5th Dimensional evolution for their collective.

Do not assume any answers. When you have that approach, you can miss growing your own knowledge. Having an open mind is very important, and this has to keep being reminded to all as the best way to grow.

Events can change quickly. We can trust that our collective is working on getting everyone the best overall experience to naturally awaken for those who have that life contract to awaken this lifetime, and for all to have the right experience for future growth from those lessons.

All life contracts are respected, and we should be responsible when using our free will to match our life purpose and mission here.

Loving yourself and everyone else is the foundational factor in being a high vibrational being here on Earth. Those who have yet to read Mastering Human are encouraged to read the book. Our collectives are telling us it is very profound, as it is their information for us to truly honor and love ourselves while we are being human. The book <u>Mastering Human</u> is from recent quantum sessions.

We are in deep gratitude to all the higher dimensional beings who have been guiding us through these profound sessions and now books for all to grow with. We are so grateful they gave us access to them through quantum sessions. These sessions are a gift for humanity to grow. Please respect these methods as the treasures they are.

There are some very limited mindsets about quantum sessions being done online. It is well documented that Dolores said to only do these sessions in person, that was said by her while she was living. Unfortunately, she had her exit point in 2014 when she did not have the support underneath her as she needed. She physically died after a fall. When we ask about this in sessions, as many clients are interested in her, she is always happy to explain what was going on for her at this time. The shift in 2012 did not happen as fear and lack of faith was still distracting humanity from loving itself and having full empowerment. When you read her books, you will read how she was telling us that her method was given to her — to us — by THEM, and that this is a living, evolving method. And she was excited to see other people grow it, and they were getting the same results as she was, being able to connect to the same higher dimensional beings. Everyone should be encouraged to read all of her original books she published, and also remember she is still very much here willing to help anyone who has the pure agenda to empower themselves and others to prepare for coming experiences including Old Earth and the shift to New Earth. This is why many have come to Earth this lifetime. The significance of this period for this planet and humanity is extremely important. As Dolores said in her books, she found clients were more comfortable in their own beds, in their own homes, and as her method is an evolving method, so too is our technology and ways of communication. Zoom, for example, became a common way of connection for many as the world changed in 2020.

Message in July 2020 about doing sessions online

(Two QHHT and BQH practitioners concerned about why QHHT was being held back from supporting people in need.)

S: We are in very troubled times that makes it very difficult for us to offer in-person QHHT sessions. There are those who think that we need to only do in-person sessions, when many times, I'm afraid, it's not going to be possible for many of us, so what would you recommend we do?

J: As I have already stated to you before, I would like you to do the sessions any way you can. We do not have time to dilly-dally around with specifics. You just need to do it! You need to do this work. You've been trained to do this work, and you now must honor this work, regardless of whether you can see the client face-to-face in-person or whether it can be done online face-to-face. You are all protected there, and we're all here to help you and the clients who need this work. I just feel frustrated that, you know, common sense hasn't been used here. While, yes, I did say that when I was alive, to not do this work online — please remember the time and the quality of technology when I said that. It has definitely changed. It is frustrating that the people that should be the most astute and proactive in evolving this the most, who should be most aware in using common sense and asking me through sessions and knowing how to ask in general questions to the oversouls who are the guardians of this planet, to see people misinterpreting me and limiting this work, is less than desirable. I did say that once at that time, that is for sure, but now when you can ask me directly through these sessions what my advice is to you, and I will say to anyone who asks the right questions to me: this work needs to be done any way it can. And I will always endorse the good practitioners who can do this work with good heart integrity, good intuition, and pure passion for this work to do it anyway they can, because they'll have the clients asking them and needing this work more than ever before.

S: So could you tell us right now, in fact, that the need is much greater than the risk?

J: Yes, absolutely. Absolutely, and the fact that people are trying to stop humanity from awakening, the fact that people are trying to stop and limit these sessions from happening. I can't fathom what the belief of that is there. It's just spiritually coasting at its finest. It is just so disappointing that this work hasn't evolved with the times. There have been other people who have taken my work and have extended it on and are very successful and very safe online. Why hasn't my QHHT done that for me, why hasn't my QHHT done that for humanity?! This work cannot be limited because of personal issues and egos.

S: So I'm new to QHHT. I have never seen the people that are in charge, but why is it that they fear to make the technique evolve into an online method?

J: The lack of trust, the lack of trust of people, the lack of trust that a stranger could meet another stranger on a computer screen and they have a deep profound connection. So profound that the person can trust and go into trance. This is so easy that it's done all the time. It's not about anything more but a lack of understanding of this work. It is disappointing that this hasn't evolved and that many people are missing out on having sessions because they are so loyal to this work. That they don't want to do anything that is against it, but no one seems to have even questioned it! No one has gone to the top and said, "Wake up! People can trust the technology has updated! This is just not Dolores' work, this is not your work— this is THEIR work!" This is the work for humanity, and whoever is blocking humanity's growth shall be speaking to me!

S: So we are working with energy when we work on the QHHT sessions right? (J: Yes) So when reiki is working with energy, they could work at a distance— so it would make sense, then, as other practices could function remotely. QHHT should be able to work remotely as well, am I right, like how BQH can?

J: Yes. The egos of some practitioners who believe that they are providing their clients with the energy are lacking understanding of this work. It is the client's higher self that gives them the energy to be able to connect and channel them. The practitioner is merely just reading the script and holding space for the questions. The practitioner isn't the magician here. The client surrenders into the process and allows themselves to connect with their higher selves, to connect with the subconscious, and to connect with other bigger beings. The client empowers themselves to do these sessions. It has got nothing to do with energy done online, that's complete nonsense.

S: Okay, and there is no danger or risk, right?

J: Well, and it's just like for people who still believe that there are negative entity attachments, those people that interfere can say that the sky is falling tomorrow, and we will all laugh at them, because it's just fear-based trouble.

You must all remember, you are multidimensional beings, you are loved, you are protected, and you are supported always. We would never ever allow anything to happen to you. You are so protected. My script protects you beyond, and people who don't understand that, don't trust this work— they should not be doing this work if they do not understand it profoundly. You need to do your own sessions, and ask these questions before putting other people's spiritual growth on hold, while you are still trying to figure out what you're actually doing here.

S: Do you think we should be sharing this advice of yours today with the QHHT community?

J: The people who want to hold onto their egos, who want to keep it small and limited, they will now feel frustrated that they've been told off by Dolores! They still feel so smart and confident because they want to quote me when I was alive, but yet, they don't want to ask me the real questions and the big questions when they can contact me in sessions! It is frustrating to me, and it's frustrating to her, and we both can't understand why there is this lack of growth and evolution with QHHT as I said in my books. The frustrating thing is that they had a lot of time to connect with each other and do practice sessions. I had hoped that the true practitioners, the ones who should shine on, would have connected with their other practitioner friends and had exchanged sessions and profoundly grown within this work.

What I said to you right at the beginning, before the lockdown is: to grow within quickly, quickly, quickly. Grow within quickly as you go. Because we all need to get you ready, for as many practitioners to be ready for being able to help when humanity changes. A lot of these practitioners, unfortunately, have been sitting on their laurels, and it is frustrating because they were being tested. They were able to have this opportunity. They were able to have all of this time to be able to go within and have some fun sessions, and test it out, and then come and ask me how I would feel about them doing sessions online. I would have been able to say to them what I have said to the vehicle and many other people who already have asked me. It is no harder to connect with the client in a different way and not just rely on body gestures or the comfort of an office. But you also can rely on the fact that they are safe and happy in their own homes, too. There are pluses and minuses with everything. I don't want you to feel that doing this work online is bad. However, this work can be done as long as the client is really, truly ready to have a session and is able to surrender and is able to connect. There doesn't have to be a practitioner in the room to do that. Technology these days allows you to connect with people much quicker and be able to have chit chats beforehand and chit chats afterwards. Don't keep carbon copying, cutting and pasting my method exactly how I did it because those times have gone! They will never come back, and the people who are holding on to that work, then are also, unfortunately, holding on to me. I have also gone from that state, and I'm here. I've always been here. And I am waiting for those people who are still struggling to move on from that— to profoundly connect to me, because I've been waiting. I have a lot of conversations to have with them.

S: Well, I thank you for having a conversation with me because I'm just a beginner in your practice. I have been very excited about this, so it is a great honor to be able to hear from you. It is wonderful to know that me being in Florida and the vehicle being in New Zealand, we could actually hold the session. I thank you for validating our work for the future. Do you have a last message for humanity today?

J: The Internet is much better than the Internet that I had, and the applications that people can use today are more reliable. There is no risk with doing online sessions at all, and the people that want to hold on to the fact that there may be risks — they've got their own work to grow and overcome. They're still afraid of the boogeyman, so to speak, so those are the people that are not truly ready to do this work, either as clients or as practitioners. In terms of the energy interference, which actually often happens with these sessions, there's nothing to be concerned about. There is some lag sometimes, and there are differences here, but we are different. Your clients are different from the clients that I had. Your clients are more aware, they're more intuitive, they've got a lot more going for them, and they can cope with this. They're not my clients. My clients may not have coped with being more aware of the information during the session, it was good most were so much more deeper, and literally did not recall anything from the sessions at all. And thanks to the shift that happened in 2012, we have grown. Humanity has grown, and I am proud of the small part that I played for humanity to be able to help with that, which makes me feel very proud of the work that I have done. But I don't want to limit this work, and it's so frustrating that there are so many people actively limiting this work. Remember, it is not the work that I created, the work created me. With the blessing of being able to connect to the super consciousness, I've been able to get the help that I needed to help humanity. It would almost be rude of practitioners to not tap into their guides to ask them how they can help humanity, just as you're asking today. You're asking the right questions, and I wish that more people took the courage and the time to do that for themselves. I say this with love, and of course, there is that ultimate statement of "Dolores would you do it now? Would you do a session online?" and I say to people: I loved connecting with you all, each and every one of my clients. I was so honored, I loved meeting you in-person and having that special time together, and I wouldn't trade that in for the world. If I had to do my time again, I would do it all again face-to-face. I'm not alive now. I don't have the luxury of that choice. You have choices now. You're adults. Don't misuse this work. You want the best for your clients, and so go and do it! You don't have much time to dilly-dally around, and you don't have much time to keep asking me the same questions! I say that with love.

S: Thank you very much, Dolores. Until next time.

J: You're welcome, ladies, and I love you and I adore you all. You're doing such good work, and you're asking the harder questions. I can't wait to be able to catch up with you all.

Important Reminder

Dolores created QHHT as a safe and protected way for clients to channel their guides for information to help them for this lifetime, which includes coming events. Anyone that would suggest dark programming information could be given to the client during QHHT sessions is not respecting or trusting the over-soul who is supporting the clients, not just during the session, but for their lifetimes. As Dolores would say, QUESTION everything and think for yourself. QHHT INTERNS support 25 people for free as part of their training. Explore these protected sessions yourself, and ask your guides many questions. Dolores' books are still important — perhaps you should ask Dolores to come into your session. Get your practitioner to ask her if she ever had dark programming come into her sessions — to see what she has to say about that. She might even want to share other helpful insights for you to also know.

BQH is another safe and protected method for people to channel in their higher self.

Anyone who is still living with fear would be dismissing our advanced guides' roles for humanity. We invite all to grow at this important time for humanity and this planet.

With love to all.

Reminders for Clients seeking Practitioners

You will be starting a life changing friendship with your practitioner. While you are spending many hours with them for your first session, most people want more than one session, so be open to having this person close in your life. You will need to trust them completely. That can be a challenge, in itself, for those people who still have inner work to do, to have basic trust of themselves and others. Notice your reactions and triggers still. Reading <u>Mastering Human</u> is a great manual for real self empowerment.

When seeking a practitioner, you should treat this as an interview- holding people accountable to fulfill their professional position is something we all should support others to do, regardless of what industry they are in. If anyone is not happy in their choice of work, not only are they doing themselves a disservice, but this also impacts others. A great question would be to ask them: why did they start doing this work? And listen to what they share.

A sure way to know if a person is meant to be doing this work is that their own subconscious confirmed this in their own sessions as a client. Most practitioners should be having regular sessions for their own inner work and knowledge seeking. If the practitioner has not asked their own subconscious this— you can offer that this be one of your questions as the client. Both practitioners and clients are meant to be empowering each other and be accountable for their own inner work. Practitioners have been known to use their clients as a way to have their own sessions, without prior permission from the clients. There is a respectful balance. Make sure both parties feel respected. Practitioners need to respect all their clients' questions before exploring anything for themselves.

A great practitioner charges a one off price for as many sessions you need to be fully supported. That takes lots of pressure off the client to be able to relax into the session, knowing they have more chances to practice this experience. A great client would apply the information from each session and grow as fast as their subconscious knows they should be.

Making sure the practitioner can place a KEYWORD in for you at the end of sessions. This gives you the access to be able to channel your subconscious within minutes for the next session. This is not connected to the practitioner. This is for the client, as the client gets to choose the word or words used to be their keyword. Therefore, any practitioner can use this keyword for the client to channel their subconscious very quickly. Many practitioners have a cheaper rate for those clients who have a keyword, and having an intern session just for the keyword is a great tool for busy practitioners who have little time for full sessions. The more sessions you have, the more relaxed and trusting of the process you will be. Therefore, find practitioners who are honestly interested in what is happening for you and your life and truly want the best for you.

What to Look for in a Practitioner

~ Interns who honestly honor doing the free 25 sessions with QHHT sessions. It does not matter what other skill sets they have that are not QHHT sessions, therefore 25 successful FREE SESSIONS with 25 different CLIENTS would be the most beneficial approach for a great foundation in this method.

~ Practitioners who empower you to keep listening to your sessions again. A great practitioner listens to your sessions as you are channeling and can empower you by reminding you of your guide's messages later down the track. Good practitioners will be wanting to support with you what your subconscious says about how to move forward in your life with the right perspectives. At times, it is hard to apply the information. Having a friend who reminds you of your purpose and life contracts is a great friend to have.

~ If the practitioner is displaying any mindsets from a fear-based/ or limited-based perspective/ opinionated approaches, your sessions will be a great way to also help them grow. Both Practitioner and Client are learning in these sessions.

~ Remembering FEAR can look like many things - anything that is holding someone back is a form of fear. Explore it in your own sessions.

~ Everyone can go into a deep trance, however, antipsychotic drugs will block this connection, as they are too open to other dimensions. This can confuse and misdiagnose them within the mental health systems.

~ Practitioners who are still learning can assume things like attached entities, for example. A great practitioner will ask many questions, and assume nothing until they have heard it from advanced beings. We know that advanced beings do not get tripped over names and labels, but the human ego can. That is when we can hear, in some practitioners' public sessions, them having their clients in very light states of trance using their egos to talk about entities, for example. When we know we are always protected and nothing can impact us, we use our free will, and create this for ourselves. Those practitioners are creating a show for entertainment, over actually supporting their clients to get to the root of the real issues and help them have the epiphanies to see what they are creating for themselves. Same can be said about those who still think retrogrades and certain dates impact us. We are not victims to planets or dates. We are only victims to our own limited mindsets throwing our empowerment away. Also, we can be powerful and have connections to our guides all the time. There is no real date which opens a portal up to be stronger or more special than any other time. Remember, time is a man-made concept, therefore, advanced beings do not have time or even work within the sense of our Earth time. That again is a human belief system, and from our collective perspectives, this way of thinking is disempowering people rather than empowering people. You are always connected to Source, and you can choose to distract yourself away from LOVE, if that is your choice to do so, so use your free will wisely :)

the SHIFT to NEW EARTH

WE love you

we LOVE you

we love YOU

the SHIFT to NEW EARTH

This is a wonderful time to empower yourself
connectingtoheaven@gmail.com

the SHIFT to NEW EARTH

Other Books from Conversations with Heaven on Earth

MASTERING OLD EARTH

MASTERING HUMAN

EXPLORE the SHIFT to NEW EARTH

Time : The Convoluted Concept of Being Human

Depressed People Don't Eat Salads

So, there's THAT

We Say This With So Much Love

We Are Here For This

Printed in Great Britain
by Amazon